CAMBRIDGE LIBRARY COLLECTION

Books of enduring scholarly value

North American History

This series includes accounts of historical events and movements by eye-witnesses and contemporaries, as well as landmark studies that assembled significant source materials or developed new historiographical methods. The works range from the writings of early U.S. Presidents to journals of poor European settlers, from travellers' descriptions of bustling cities and vast landscapes to critiques of racial inequality and descriptions of Native American culture under threat of annihilation. The commercial, political and social aspirations and rivalries of the 'new world' are reflected in these fascinating eighteenth- and nineteenth-century publications.

Observations on the Importance of the American Revolution

Having urged political reforms in Britain, Richard Price (1723–91) turned to defending the cause of American independence. Born in Wales, Price became an influential moral philosopher, dissenting Protestant preacher, political pamphleteer, and economic theorist. Known for his trenchant defence of the freedom of the human will against philosophical sceptics, Price applied his justification of individual moral agency to political issues – particularly the American Revolution – during the latter part of his life. This tract on America first appeared in 1784. Defining the right of American colonists to oppose British corruption, it suggested that their independence would offer much 'benefit to the world'. But it also offered a relatively rare critique of the system of racial slavery that continued to develop in America. Reissued here is the 1785 publication that also contained translations from French of a letter to Price by the economist Turgot and a parody by Charles-Joseph Mathon de la Cour which had amused Benjamin Franklin.

Cambridge University Press has long been a pioneer in the reissuing of out-of-print titles from its own backlist, producing digital reprints of books that are still sought after by scholars and students but could not be reprinted economically using traditional technology. The Cambridge Library Collection extends this activity to a wider range of books which are still of importance to researchers and professionals, either for the source material they contain, or as landmarks in the history of their academic discipline.

Drawing from the world-renowned collections in the Cambridge University Library and other partner libraries, and guided by the advice of experts in each subject area, Cambridge University Press is using state-of-the-art scanning machines in its own Printing House to capture the content of each book selected for inclusion. The files are processed to give a consistently clear, crisp image, and the books finished to the high quality standard for which the Press is recognised around the world. The latest print-on-demand technology ensures that the books will remain available indefinitely, and that orders for single or multiple copies can quickly be supplied.

The Cambridge Library Collection brings back to life books of enduring scholarly value (including out-of-copyright works originally issued by other publishers) across a wide range of disciplines in the humanities and social sciences and in science and technology.

Observations on the Importance of the American Revolution

RICHARD PRICE

CAMBRIDGE
UNIVERSITY PRESS

CAMBRIDGE UNIVERSITY PRESS

Cambridge, New York, Melbourne, Madrid, Cape Town,
Singapore, São Paolo, Delhi, Mexico City

Published in the United States of America by Cambridge University Press, New York

www.cambridge.org
Information on this title: www.cambridge.org/9781108060172

© in this compilation Cambridge University Press 2013

This edition first published 1785
This digitally printed version 2013

ISBN 978-1-108-06017-2 Paperback

OBSERVATIONS

ON THE

IMPORTANCE

OF THE

AMERICAN REVOLUTION,

AND

The MEANS of making it a BENEFIT to the WORLD.

TO WHICH IS ADDED,

A LETTER from M. TURGOT, late Comptroller-General of the Finances of France:

WITH

An APPENDIX, containing a Tranflation of the WILL of M. FORTUNÉ RICARD, lately publifhed in *France*.

―――――――

By RICHARD PRICE, D.D. L.L.D.

And FELLOW of the ROYAL SOCIETY of LONDON, and of the ACADEMY of ARTS and SCIENCES in NEW-ENGLAND.

―――――――

LONDON:

Printed for T. CADELL, in the STRAND.

M.DCC.LXXXV.

TO

The FREE AND UNITED STATES OF
AMERICA,

THE FOLLOWING OBSERVATIONS

ARE HUMBLY OFFERED,

AS

A LAST TESTIMONY

OF

THE GOOD - WILL

OF

THE AUTHOR.

[v]

CONTENTS.

ADVERTISEMENT.

HAVING reason to hope I should be attended to in the American States, and thinking I saw an opening there favourable to the improvement and best interests of mankind, I have been induced to convey thither the sentiments and advice contained in the following Observations. They were, therefore, originally intended only for America. The danger of a spurious edition has now obliged me to publish them in my own country.

I should be inexcusable did I not take this opportunity to express my gratitude to a distinguished writer (the Count de Mirabeau) for his translation of these Observations into French, and for the support and kind civility with which it has been accompanied.

Mr. Turgot's letter formed a part of this tract when it was conveyed to America. I have now given a translation of it.

I think

*I think it necessary to add that I have ex-
pressed myself in some respects too strongly in the*
conclusion *of the following* Observations. *By
accounts from persons the best informed, I have
lately been assured that no such dissentions exist
among the American States as have been given
out in this country; that the new governments
are in general well settled, and the people happy under them; and that, in particular, a
conviction is becoming universal of the necessity
of giving more strength to that power which
forms and which is to conduct and maintain
their union.*

March, 1785.

OBSER-

OBSERVATIONS, &c.

Of the IMPORTANCE *of the* REVOLUTION
*which has eſtabliſhed the Independence of
the United States.*

HAVING, from pure conviction, taken
a warm part in favour of the *Britiſh*
colonies (now the United States of America) during the late war; and been expoſed,
in conſequence of this, to *much* abuſe and
ſome danger; it muſt be ſuppoſed that I
have been waiting for the iſſue with anxiety —— I am thankful that my anxiety
is removed; and that I have been ſpared to
be a witneſs to that very iſſue of the war
which has been all along the object of my
wiſhes. With heart-felt ſatisfaction, I ſee
the revolution in favour of univerſal liberty
which has taken place in *America*;—a revolution which opens a new proſpect in hu-

B   man

man affairs, and begins a new æra in the hiftory of mankind ;——a revolution by which *Britons* themfelves will be the greateft gainers, if wife enough to improve properly the check that has been given to the defpotifm of their minifters, and to catch the flame of virtuous liberty which has faved their American brethren.

The late war, in its *commencement and progrefs*, did great good by diffeminating juft fentiments of the rights of mankind, and the nature of legitimate government; by exciting a fpirit of refiftance to tyranny which has emancipated one *European* country, and is likely to emancipate others ; and by occafioning the eftablifhment in *America* of forms of government more equitable and more liberal than any that the world has yet known. But, in its *termination*, the war has done ftill greater good by preferving the new governments from that deftruction in which they muft have been involved, had Britain conquered ; by providing, in a fequeftered continent poffeffed of many fingular advantages, a place of refuge for oppreft men in every region of the world ; and by laying the foundation there

of

of an empire which may be the feat of liberty, fcience and virtue, and from whence there is reafon to hope thefe facred bleffings will fpread, till they become univerfal, and the time arrives when kings and priefts fhall have no more power to opprefs, and that ignominious flavery which has hitherto debafed the world is exterminated. I therefore, think I fee the hand of Providence in the late war working for the general good.

Reafon, as well as tradition and revelation, lead us to expect that a more improved and happy ftate of human affairs will take place before the confummation of all things. The world has hitherto been gradually improving. Light and knowledge have been gaining ground, and human life *at prefent* compared with what it *once* was, is much the fame that a youth approaching to manhood is compared with an infant.

Such are the natures of things that this progrefs muft continue. During particular intervals it may be interrupted, but it cannot be deftroy'd. Every prefent advance prepares the way for farther advances; and a fingle experiment or difcovery may fome-

times

times give rife to fo many more as fuddenly
to raife the fpecies higher, and to refemble
the effects of opening a new fenfe, or of the
fall of a fpark on a train that fprings a mine.
For this reafon, mankind may at laft arrive
at degrees of improvement which we cannot now even fufpect to be poffible. A
dark age may follow an enlightened age;
but, in this cafe, the light, after being
fmothered for a time, will break out again
with a brighter luftre. The prefent age of
increafed light, confidered as fucceeding the
ages of *Greece* and *Rome* and an interme-
diate period of thick darknefs, furnifhes a
proof of the truth of this obfervation.
There are certain kinds of improvement
which, when once made, cannot be entirely loft. During the dark ages, the improvements made in the ages that preceded
them remained fo far as to be recovered immediately at the refurrection of letters, and
to produce afterwards that more rapid progrefs in improvement which has diftinguifhed modern times.

There can fcarcely be a more pleafing and
encouraging object of reflection than this.
An accidental obfervation of the effects
of gravity in a garden has been the means

of

of difcovering the laws that govern the
folar fyftem*, and of enabling us to look
down with pity on the ignorance of the
moft enlightened times among the antients.
What new dignity has been given to man,
and what additions have been made to his
powers, by the invention of optical glaffes,
printing, gun-powder, &c. and by the late
difcoveries in navigation, mathematics, natural philofophy, &c. ? †

* This refers to an account given of Sir Ifaac Newton in the Preface to Dr. PEMBERTON's View of his
Philofophy.

† Who could have thought, in the firft ages of the
world, that mankind would acquire the power of determining the diftances and magnitudes of the fun and
planets ?—Who, even at the beginning of this century,
would have thought, that, in a few years, mankind
would acquire the power of fubjecting to their wills the
dreadful force of lightening, and of flying in aeroftatic
machines ?—The laft of thefe powers, though fo long
undifcovered, is only an eafy application of a power always known.—Many fimilar difcoveries may remain to
be made, which will give new directions of the greateft
confequence to human affairs; and it may not be too
extravagant to expect that (fhould civil governments
throw no obftacles in the way) the progrefs of improvement will not ceafe till it has excluded from the earth
moft of its worft evils, and reftored that Paradifaical
ftate which, according to the Mofaic Hiftory, preceded
the prefent ftate.

But

But among the events in modern times tending to the elevation of mankind, there are none probably of so much confequence as the recent one which occafions thefe obfervations. Perhaps, I do not go too far when I fay that, next to the introduction of Chriftianity among mankind, the American revolution may prove the moft important ftep in the progreffive courfe of human improvement. It is an event which may produce a general diffufion of the principles of humanity, and become the means of fetting free mankind from the fhackles of fuperftition and tyranny, by leading them to fee and know " that nothing " is *fundamental* but impartial enquiry, an " honeft mind, and virtuous practice ——— " that ftate policy ought not to be applied " to the fupport of fpeculative opinions " and formularies of faith."——" That the " members of a civil community are * *con-* " *federates,* not *fubjects*; and their rulers, " *fervants,* not *mafters.* —— And that all " legitimate government confifts in the do- " minion of equal laws made with com- " mon confent; that is, in the dominion

---

* Thefe are the words of MONTESQUIEU.

" of

" of men over *themselves*; and not in the
" dominion of communities over commu-
" nities, or of any men over other men."

Happy will the world be when these truths shall be every where acknowledged and practised upon. Religious bigotry, that cruel demon, will be then laid asleep. Slavish governments and slavish Hierarchies will then sink; and the old prophecies be verified, " that the last universal empire
" upon earth shall be the empire of reason
" and virtue, under which the gospel of
" peace (better understood) *shall have free*
" *course and be glorified, many will run to*
" *and fro and knowledge be increased, the*
" *wolf dwell with the lamb and the leopard*
" *with the kid, and nation no more lift up*
" *a sword against nation.*"

It is a conviction I cannot resist, that the independence of the *English* colonies in America is one of the steps ordained by Providence to introduce these times; and I can scarcely be deceived in this convic-tion, if the United States should escape some dangers which threaten them, and will take proper care to throw themselves open to future improvements, and to make the most of the advantages of their present
fituation.

fituation. Should this happen, it will be true of them as it was of the people of the Jews, that *in them all the families of the earth ſhall be bleſſed.* It is ſcarcely poſſible they ſhould think too highly of their own conſequence. Perhaps, there never exiſted a people on whoſe wiſdom and virtue more depended; or to whom a ſtation of more importance in the plan of Providence has been aſſigned. They have begun nobly. They have fought with ſuccefs for themſelves and for the world; and, in the midſt of invaſion and carnage, eſtabliſhed forms of government favourable in the higheſt degree to the rights of mankind. —— But they have much more to do; more indeed than it is poſſible properly to repreſent. In this addreſs, my deſign is only to take notice of a few *great* points which ſeem particularly to require their attention, in order to render them permanently happy in themſelves and uſeful to mankind. On theſe points, I ſhall deliver my ſentiments with freedom, conſcious I mean well; but, at the ſame time, with real diffidence, conſcious of my own liablenefs to error.

Of

Of the Means of promoting human Improvement and Happiness in the United States. —And first, of Public Debts.

IT seems evident, that what first requires the attention of the United States is the redemption of their debts, and making compensation to that army which has carried them through the war. They have an infant credit to cherish and rear, which, if this is not done, must perish, and with it their character and honour for ever. Nor is it conceivable they should meet with any great difficulties in doing this. They have a vast resource peculiar to themselves, in a continent of unlocated lands possessing every advantage of soil and climate. The settlement of these lands will be rapid, the consequence of which must be a rapid increase of their value. By disposing of them to the army and to emigrants, the greatest part of the debts of the United States may probably be sunk *immediately*. But had they no such resource, they are very capable of bearing taxes sufficient for the purpose of a gradual redemption. Sup-

C

poſing their debts to amount to *nine millions* sterling, carrying intereſt at $5\frac{1}{2}$ *per cent*. taxes producing a revenue of a million *per ann.* would pay the intereſt, and at the ſame time leave a *ſurplus* of *half* a million *per ann.* for a *ſinking fund*, which would diſcharge the principal in thirteen years. A ſurplus of a *quarter* of a million would do the ſame in $20\frac{1}{2}$ years. After diſcharging the principal, the appropriated revenue being no longer wanted, might be aboliſhed, and the States eaſed of the burthen of it. But it would be imprudent to aboliſh it entirely. 100,000 *l. per ann.* reſerved, and faithfully laid out in clearing unlocated lands and other improvements, would in a ſhort time increaſe to a treaſure (or continental patrimony) which would defray the whole expenditure of the union, and keep the States free from debts and taxes for ever*. Such a *reſerve* would (ſup-

---

* The lands, foreſts, impoſts, &c. &c. which once formed the *patrimony* of the crown in *England*, bore moſt of the expences of government. It is well for this kingdom that the extravagance of the crown has been the means of alienating this patrimony, for the conſequence has been making the crown dependent on the people. But in America ſuch a patrimony would be *continental* property, capable of being applied only to public purpoſes, in the way which the public (or its delegates) would approve.

poſing

poſing it improved ſo as to produce a
profit of 5 *per cent.*) increaſe to a capital
of three millions in 19 years, 30 millions
in 57 years, 100 millions in 81 yesrs, and
261 millions in 100 years. But ſuppoſing
it capable of being improved ſo as to
produce a profit of 10 *per cent.* it would
increaſe to five millions in 19 years, 100
millions in 49 years, and 10,000 millions
in 97 years.

It is wonderful that no ſtate has yet
thought of taking this method to make
itſelf great and rich. The ſmalleſt appro-
priation in a ſinking fund, *never diverted*,
operates in cancelling debts, juſt as money
increaſes at compound intereſt; and is,
therefore, *omnipotent* *. But, if *diverted*,
it loſes all its power. BRITAIN affords
a ſtriking proof of this. Its ſinking fund
(once the hope of the kingdom) has, by

---

* One penny put out at our Saviour's birth to 5 *per
cent.* compound intereſt would, before this time, have
increaſed to a greater ſum than would be contained in
TWO HUNDRED MILLIONS of EARTHS all ſolid gold.
But, if put out to *ſimple* intereſt, it would have amount-
ed to no more than *ſeven ſhillings and ſix-pence.* All
governments which alienate *funds* deſtined for reim-
burſements, chuſe to improve money in the *laſt* rather
than the *firſt* of theſe ways.

the

the practice of alienating it, been rendered impotent and ufelefs. Had it been inviolably applied to the purpofe for which it was intended, there would, in the year 1775, have been a *furplus* in the revenue of more than five millions *per ann*. But inftead of this, we were then encumbered with a debt of 137 millions, carrying an intereft of near 4½ millions, and leaving no furplus of any confequence. This debt has been fince increafed to * 280 millions, carrying an intereft (including expences of management) of *nine* millions and a half.——A monftrous bubble ;—and if no very ftrong meafures are foon taken to reduce it within the limits of fafety, it muft produce a dreadful convulfion. Let the United States take warning—Their debts at prefent are moderate. A Sinking fund, guarded † againft mifapplication, may foon extinguifh them, and prove a refource in all events of the greateft importance.

* See the *Poftfcript* to a pamphlet, entitled, *The State of the Finances of the Kingdom, at figning the Preliminary Articles of Peace* in January 1783, printed for Mr. Cadell.

† When not thus guarded, public funds become the worft evils, by giving to the rulers of ftates a command of revenue for the purpofes of corruption.

I muft

I muſt not, however, forget that there is ONE of their debts on which no ſinking fund can have any effect; and which it is impoſſible for them to diſcharge: —— A debt, greater, perhaps, than has been ever due from any country; and which will be deeply felt by their lateſt poſterity. —But it is a debt of GRATITUDE only— Of GRATITUDE to that General, who has been raiſed up by Providence to make them free and independent, and whoſe name muſt ſhine among the firſt in the future annals of the benefactors of mankind.

The meaſure now propoſed may preſerve America for ever from too great an accumulation of debts; and, conſequently, of taxes—an evil which is likely to be the ruin not only of *Britain*, but of other *European* States.—But there are meaſures of yet greater conſequence, which I wiſh ardently to recommend and inculcate.

For the ſake of mankind, I wiſh to ſee every meaſure adopted that can have a tendency to preſerve PEACE in America; and to make it an open and fair ſtage for diſcuſſion, and the ſeat of PERFECT LIBERTY.

Of

Of PEACE,

And the Means of perpetuating it.

CIVIL GOVERNMENT is an expedient for collecting the wifdom and force of a community or confederacy, in order to preferve its peace and liberty againft every hoftile invafion, whether from *within* or from *without.*—In the latter of thefe refpects, the United States are happily fecured; but they are far from being equally happy in the *former* refpect. Having now, in confequence of their fuccefsful refiftance of the invafion of *Britain*, united to their remotenefs from *Europe*, no external enemy to fear, they are in danger of fighting with one another.—This is their *greateft* danger; and providing fecurities againft it is their *hardeft* work. Should they fail in this, America may fome time or other be turned into a fcene of blood; and inftead of being the hope and refuge of the world, may become a terror to it.

When a difpute arifes among *individuals* in a State, an appeal is made to a *court* of

law;

law; that is, to the wifdom and juftice of the State. The court decides. The lofing party acquiefces; or, if he does not, the power of the State *forces* him to fubmiffion; and thus the effects of contention are fuppreft, and peace is maintained.—In a way fimilar to this, peace may be maintained between any number of confederated States; and I can almoft imagine, that it is not impoffible but that by fuch means *univerfal* peace may be produced, and all war excluded from the world.—Why may we not hope to fee this begun in America?——The articles of confederation make confiderable advances towards it. When a difpute arifes between any of the States, they order an appeal to Congrefs, —an enquiry by Congrefs,—a hearing,— and a decifion.—But here they ftop.—What is moft of all neceffary is omitted. No provifion is made for enforcing the decifions of Congrefs; and this renders them inefficient and futile. I am by no means qualified to point out the beft method of removing this defect. Much muft be given up for this purpofe, nor is it eafy to give up *too* much. Without all doubt the

powers

powers of Congrefs muft be enlarged. In
particular, a power muft be given it to
collect, on certain emergencies, the force
of the confederacy, and to employ it in
carrying its decifions into execution. A
State againft which a decifion is made, will
yield of courfe when it knows that fuch a
force exifts, and that it allows no hope
from refiftance.

By this force I do not mean a STANDING
ARMY. God forbid, that ftanding armies
fhould ever find an eftablifhment in America. They are every where the grand
fupports of arbitrary power, and the chief
caufes of the depreffion of mankind. No
wife people will truft their defence out of
their own hands, or confent to hold their
rights at the mercy of armed *flaves*. Free
States ought to be bodies of armed *citizens*,
well regulated, and well difciplined, and
always ready to turn out, when properly
called upon, to execute the laws, to quell
riots, and to keep the peace. Such, if I
am rightly informed, are the citizens of
America. Why then may not CONGRESS
be furnifhed with a power of calling out
from the confederated States, *quotas* of
militia fufficient to force at once the compliance

pliance of any State which may fhew an inclination to break the union by refifting its decifions ?

I am very fenfible that it will be diffi-cult to guard fuch a power againft abufe ; and, perhaps, better means of anfwering this end are difcoverable. In human af-fairs, however, the choice generally offered us is " of two evils to take the leaft." We chufe the reftraint of civil govern-ment, becaufe a lefs evil than anarchy; and, in like manner, in the prefent in-ftance, the danger of the abufe of power, and of its being employed fometimes to enforce wrong decifions, muft be fubmitted to, becaufe a lefs evil than the mifery of inteftine wars. Much, however, may be done to leffen this danger. Such regula-tions as thofe in the ninth of the articles of confederation will, in a great meafure, pre-vent hafty and partial decifions. The ro-tation eftablifhed by the fifth article will prevent that corruption of character which feldom fails to be produced by the long poffeffion of power ; and the right referved to every State of recalling its Delegates when diffatisfied with them, will keep them conftantly refponfible and cautious.

D   The

The obfervations now made muft be extended to money tranfactions. Congrefs muft be trufted with a power of procuring fupplies for defraying the expences of the confederation ; of contracting debts, and providing funds for difcharging them : and this power muft not be capable of being defeated by the oppofition of any minority in the States.

In fhort, the credit of the United States, their ftrength, their refpectablenefs abroad, their liberty at home, and even their exiftence, depend on the prefervation of a firm political union; and fuch an union cannot be preferved, without giving all poffible weight and energy to the authority of that delegation which conftitutes the union.

Would it not be proper to take periodical furveys of the different ftates, their numbers of both fexes in every ftage of life, their condition, occupations, property, &c. ?——Would not fuch furveys, in conjunction with accurate regifters of births, marriages and deaths at all ages, afford much important inftruction by fhew-

3   ing

ing what laws govern human mortality, and
what fituations, employments, and civil
inftitutions, are moft favourable to the
health and happinefs of mankind ?———
Would they not keep conftantly in view
the progrefs of population in the ftates, and
the increafe or decline of their refources?
But more efpecially, are they not the only
means of procuring the neceffary information for determining accurately and equita-
bly the proportions of men and money to
be contributed by each ftate for fupporting
and ftrengthening the confederation ?

D 2   *Of*

Of LIBERTY.

THE next point I would infift on, as an object of fupreme importance, is the eftablifhment of fuch a fyftem of perfect liberty, *religious* as well as *civil*, in America, as fhall render it a country where truth and reafon fhall have fair play, and the human powers find full fcope for exerting themfelves, and for fhewing how far they can carry human improvement.

The faculties of man have hitherto, in all countries, been more or lefs cramped by the interference of civil authority in matters of fpeculation, by tyrannical laws againft herefy and fchifm, and by flavifh hierarchies and religious eftablifhments. It is above all things defirable that no fuch fetters on reafon fhould be admitted into America. I obferve, with inexpreffible fatisfaction, that at prefent they have no exiftence there. In this refpect the governments of the United States are liberal to a degree that is unparalleled. They have the diftinguifhed honour of being the firft

ftates

ſtates under heaven in which forms of government have been eſtabliſhed favourable
to *univerſal* liberty. They have been thus
diſtinguiſhed in their *infancy*. What then
will they be in a more advanced ſtate;
when time and experience, and the concurring aſſiſtance of the wiſe and virtuous in
every part of the earth, ſhall have introduced into the new governments, corrections and amendments which will render
them ſtill more friendly to liberty, and
more the means of promoting human happineſs and dignity? —— May we not ſee
there the dawning of brighter days on
earth, and a new creation riſing. But I
muſt check myſelf. I am in danger of being carried too far by the ardor of my
hopes.

The liberty I mean includes in it liberty
of conduct in all *civil* matters—liberty
of diſcuſſion in all *ſpeculative* matters—and
liberty of conſcience in all *religious* matters.——And it is then *perfect*, when under no reſtraint except when uſed to injure
any one in his perſon, property, or good
name; that is, except when uſed to deſtroy
itſelf.

In

In liberty of difcuffion, I include the
liberty of examining all public meafures,
and the conduct of all public men; and of
writing and publifhing on all fpeculative
and doctrinal points.

Of LIBERTY *of* DISCUSSION.

IT is a common opinion, that there are
fome doctrines fo facred, and others of
fo bad a tendency, that no public difcuffion
of them ought to be allowed. Were this a
right opinion, all the perfecution that has
been ever practifed would be juftified. For,
if it is a part of the duty of civil magiftrates
to prevent the difcuffion of fuch doctrines,
they muft, in doing this, act on their own
judgments of the nature and tendency of
doctrines; and, confequently, they muft
have a right to prevent the difcuffion of
all doctrines which they think to be too facred for difcuffion or too dangerous in their
tendency; and this right they muft exercife in the only way in which civil power
is capable of exercifing it, " by inflicting
" penalties

" penalties on all who oppofe facred doc-
" trines, or who maintain pernicious opi-
" nions." —— In *Mahometan* countries,
therefore, civil magiftrates have a right to
filence and punifh all who oppofe the divine miffion of *Mahomet*, a doctrine *there*
reckoned of the moft facred nature. The
like is true of the doctrines of tranfubftan-
tiation, worfhip of the Virgin Mary, &c.
in *Popifh* countries ; and of the doctrines of
the Trinity, fatisfaction, &c. in *Proteftant*
countries.——In *England* itfelf, this principle has been acted upon, and produced
the laws which fubject to fevere penalties
all who write or fpeak againft the Su-
preme Divinity of Chrift, the Book of
Common Prayer, and the Church Articles
of Faith. All fuch laws are right, if the
opinion I have mentioned is right. But
in reality, civil power has nothing to do
with any fuch matters ; and civil governors go miferably out of their proper province, whenever they take upon them the
care of truth, or the fupport of any doctrinal points. They are not judges of
truth ; and if they pretend to decide about
it, they will decide wrong This all the
countries under heaven think of the application

plication of civil power to doctrinal points in every country but their own. It is, indeed, fuperftition, idolatry, and nonfenfe, that civil power at prefent fupports almoft every where, under the idea of fupporting facred truth, and oppofing dangerous error. Would not, therefore, its perfect neutrality be the greateft blefling? Would not the intereft of truth gain unfpeakably, were all the rulers of States to aim at nothing but keeping the peace; or did they confider themfelves as bound to take care, not of the *future*, but the *prefent* intereft of men ;— not of their *fouls* and their *faith*, but of their *perfons* and *property*;—not of any *ecclefiaftical*, but *fecular* matters only ?

All the experience of paft time proves that the confequence of allowing civil power to judge of the nature and tendency of doctrines, muft be making it a hindrance to the progrefs of truth, and an enemy to the improvement of the world.

Anaxagoras was tried and condemned in Greece for teaching that the fun and ftars were not Deities, but maffes of corruptible matter. Accufations of a like kind contributed to the death of *Socrates*. The threats of bigots and the fear of perfecution,

tion, prevented *Copernicus* from publish-
ing, during his whole life-time, his difcovery of the true fyftem of the world. *Ga-
lileo* was obliged to renounce the doctrine
of the motion of the earth, and fuffered a
year's imprifonment for having afferted it.
And fo lately as the year 1742, the beft
commentary on the firft production of human genius (NEWTON's *Principia)* was
not allowed to be printed at ROME, becaufe
it afferted this doctrine ; and the learned
commentators were obliged to prefix to
their work a declaration, that on this point
they fubmitted to the decifions of the fupreme Pontiffs. Such *have* been, and fuch
(while men continue blind and ignorant)
will always be the confequences of the in-
terpofition of civil governments in matters
of fpeculation.

When men affociate for the purpofe of
civil government, they do it, not to defend
truth or to fupport formularies of faith
and fpeculative opinions ; but to defend
their civil rights, and to protect one another in the free exercife of their mental
and corporeal powers. The interference,
therefore, of civil authority in fuch cafes

E   is

is directly contrary to the end of its inftitution. The way in which it can beft
promote the intereft and dignity of mankind, (as far as they can be promoted
by the difcovery of truth) is, by encouraging them to fearch for truth where-
ever they can find it; and by protecting
them in doing this againft the attacks of
malevolence and bigotry. Should any attempt be made by contending fects to injure one another, its power will come in
properly to crufh the attempt, and to maintain for all fects equal liberty, by punifhing
every encroachment upon it. The conduct of a civil magiftrate, on fuch an occafion, fhould be that of *Gallio* the wife
Roman proconful, who, on receiving an
accufation of the apoftle Paul, would not
liften to it, but drove from his prefence the
accufers who had laid violent hands upon
him, after giving them the following ad-
monition :—*If it were a matter of wrong
or wicked lewdnefs, reafon would require that
I fhould bear with you. But if it be a queftion of words and names and the law, look
you to it. For I will be no judge of fuch
matters.* Acts xviii. 12. &c. How much
happier would the world have been, had
all magiftrates acted in this manner? Let

Ame-

America learn this important leſſon, and profit by the experience of paſt times. A diſſent from *eſtabliſhed* opinions and doctrines has indeed often miſerably diſturbed ſociety, and produced miſchief and bloodſhed. But it ſhould be remembered, that this has been owing to the *eſtabliſhment* of the points diſſented from, and the uſe of civil power to enforce the reception of them. Had civil government done its duty, left all free, and employed itſelf in *procuring* inſtead of *reſtraining* fair diſcuſſion, all miſchief would have been avoided, and mankind would have been raiſed higher than they are in knowledge and improvement.

When Chriſtianity, that firſt and beſt of all the means of human improvement, was firſt preached, it was charged with turning the world upſide down. The leaders of Jewiſh and Pagan eſtabliſhments were alarmed, and by oppoſing the propagation of it, converted a religion of peace and love into an occaſion of violence and ſlaughter ; and thus verified our Lord's prophecy, that he was come *not to ſend peace, but a ſword on earth.* All this was the effect of the miſapplication

of

of the powers of government. Inftead of *creating*, they fhould have been employed in *preventing* fuch mifchief, and been *active* only in caufing the Chriftian caufe to receive a fair hearing, and guarding the propagators of it againft infult.—The like obfervation may be made concerning the firft reformers.—What we all fee would have been right in *Pagan* and *Popifh* governments with refpect to Chriftianity and the Reformation; would it not be *now* right in *Chriftian* or *Proteftant* governments, were any attempts made to propagate a new religion, or any doctrines advanced oppofite to thofe now held facred? Such attempts, if unfupported by reafon and evidence, would foon come to nothing. An impofture cannot ftand the teft of fair and open examination. On the contrary, the caufe of truth will certainly be ferved by it. *Mahometanifm* would have funk as foon as it rofe, had no other force than that of evidence been employed to propagate it; and it is an unfpeakable recommendation of *Chriftianity*, that it made its way till it became the religion of the world in one of its moft enlightened periods, by evidence only, in oppofition to the ftrongeft exertions
tions

tions of civil power. There cannot be a more ſtriking proof, that nothing but fair diſcuſſion is neceſſary to ſupprefs error and to propagate truth. I am grieved, indeed, whenever I find any Chriſtians ſhewing a diſpoſition to call in the aid of civil power to defend their religion. Nothing can be more diſgraceful to it. If it wants ſuch aid, it cannot be of God. Its corruption and debaſement took place from the moment that civil power took it under its patronage; and this corruption and debaſement increaſed, till at laſt it was converted into a ſyſtem of abſurdity and ſuperſtition more groſs and more barbarous than Paganiſm itſelf.——The religion of Chriſt diſclaims all connexion with the civil eſtabliſhments of the world. It has ſuffered infinitely by their *friendſhip*. Inſtead of ſilencing its opponents, let them be encouraged to produce their ſtrongeſt arguments againſt it. The experience of *Britain* has lately ſhewn that this will only cauſe it to be better underſtood and more firmly believed.

I would extend theſe obſervations to all points of faith, however ſacred they may

be

be deemed. Nothing reasonable can suffer by discussion. All doctrines *really* sacred must be clear and incapable of being opposed with success. If civil authority interposes, it will be to support some misconception or abuse of them.

That *immoral tendency* of doctrines which has been urged as a reason against allowing the public discussion of them, must be either *avowed* and *direct*, or only a *consequence* with which they are charged. If it is *avowed* and *direct*, such doctrines certainly will not spread. The principles rooted in human nature will resist them; and the advocates of them will be soon disgraced. If, on the contrary, it is only a *consequence* with which a doctrine is charged, it should be considered how apt all parties are to charge the doctrines they oppose with bad tendencies. It is well known, that *Calvinists* and *Arminians*, *Trinitarians* and *Socinians*, *Fatalists* and *Free-willers*, are continually exclaiming against one another's opinions as dangerous and licentious. Even Christianity itself could not, at its first introduction, escape this accusation. The professors of it were considered as *Atheists*, because they opposed Pagan idolatry; and their

their religion was on this account reckoned
a deftructive and pernicious enthufiafm.
If, therefore, the rulers of a State are to
prohibit the propagation of all doctrines in
which *they* apprehend immoral tendencies,
an opening will be made, as I have before
obferved, for every fpecies of perfecution.
There will be no doctrine, however true or
important, the avowal of which will not in
fome country or other be fubjected to civil
penalties. — Undoubtedly, there *are* doctrines which have fuch tendencies. But
the tendencies of fpeculative opinions have
often very little effect on practice. The
Author of nature has planted in the human
mind principles and feelings which will
operate in oppofition to any *theories* that
may feem to contradict them. Every fect,
whatever may be its tenets, has fome *falvo*
for the neceffity of virtue. The philofophers who hold that matter and motion
have no exiftence except in our own ideas,
are capable of believing this only in their
clofets. The fame is true of the philofophers who hold that nothing exifts *but*
matter and motion ; and at the fame time
teach, **that man** has no felf-determining
power ;

power; that an unalterable fate governs all things; and that no one *is* any thing that he can avoid *being,* or *does* any thing that he can avoid *doing.*——Thefe philofophers when they come out into the world act as other men do. Common fenfe never fails to get the better of their theories; and I know that many of them are fome of the beft as well as the ableft men in the world, and the warmeft friends to the true interefts of fociety. Though their doctrine may feem to furnifh an apology for vice, their practice is an exhibition of virtue; and a government which would filence them would greatly injure itfelf.—— Only overt acts of injuftice, violence or defamation, come properly under the cognizance of civil power. Were a perfon now to go about London, teaching that " pro- " perty is founded in grace," I fhould, were I a magiftrate, let him alone while he did nothing but *teach,* without being under any other apprehenfion than that he would foon find a lodging in *Bedlam.* But were he to attempt to carry his doctrine into its confequences by actually *ftealing,* under the pretence of his right as a faint to the property of his neighbours, I fhould

think

think it my duty to lay hold of him as a felon, without regarding the opinion from which he acted.

I am perfuaded, that few or no inconveniencies would arife from fuch a liberty. If magiftrates will do their duty as foon as violence begins, or any overt acts which break the peace are committed, no great harm will arife from their *keeping themfelves neutral* till then. Let, however, the contrary be fuppofed. Let it be granted that civil authority will in this cafe often be too *late* in its exertions; the juft inference will be, not that the liberty I plead for ought not to be allowed; but that there will be two evils, between which an option muft be made, and the leaft of which muft be preferred.——*One* is, the evil juft mentioned.——The *other* includes in it every evil which can arife from making the rulers of States judges of the tendency of doctrines, fubjecting freedom of enquiry to the controul of their ignorance, and perpetuating darknefs, intolerance and flavery. I need not fay which of thefe evils is the leaft.

F

Of LIBERTY of CONSCIENCE, and CIVIL ESTABLISHMENTS of RELIGION.

IN LIBERTY of CONSCIENCE I include much more than *Toleration*. Jesus Christ has established a perfect equality among his followers. His command is, that they shall assume no jurisdiction over one another, and acknowledge no master besides *himself.*——It is, therefore, presumption in any of them to claim a right to any superiority or pre-eminence over their brethren. Such a claim is implied, whenever any of them pretend to *tolerate* the rest.——Not only all *Christians*, but all *men* of all religions ought to be considered by a State as equally entitled to its protection as far as they demean themselves honestly and peaceably. *Toleration* can take place only where there is a civil establishment of a particular mode of religion ; that is, where a predominant sect enjoys *exclusive* advantages, and makes the encouragement of its own mode of faith and worship a part of the constitution of the State ; but at the same

I

time

time thinks fit to SUFFER the exercife of other modes of faith and worfhip. Thanks be to God, the new American States are at prefent ftrangers to fuch eftablifhments. In this refpect, as well as many others, they have fhewn, in framing their conftitutions, a degree of wifdom and liberality which is above all praife.

Civil eftablifhments of formularies of faith and worfhip are inconfiftent with the rights of private judgment—They ingender ftrife—They turn religion into a trade— They fhoar up error—They produce hypocrify and prevarication — They lay an undue byafs on the human mind in its enquiries, and obftruct the progrefs of truth.——*Genuine* religion is a concern that lies entirely between God and our own fouls. It is incapable of receiving any aid from human laws. It is contaminated as foon as worldly motives and fanctions mix their influence with it. Statefmen fhould countenance it only by exhibiting in their own example a confcientious regard to it in thofe forms which are moft agreeable to their own judgments, and by encouraging their fellow-citizens in doing the fame. They cannot as *public men* give

it

it any *other* affiftance. All befides that
has been called a *public leading* in religion,
has done it an effential injury, and produced fome of the worft confequences.

The Church Eftablifhment in *England* is
one of the mildeft and beft fort.   But even
here what a fnare has it been to integrity ?
And what a check to free enquiry ?
What difpofitions favourable to defpotifm
has it foftered ?   What a turn to pride
and narrownefs and domination has it
given the clerical character ? What ftrug-
gles has it produced in its members to
accommodate their opinions to the fub-
fcriptions and tefts which it impofes ? What
a perverfion of learning has it occafioned
to defend obfelete creeds and abfurdities ?
What a burthen is it on the confciences of
fome of its beft clergy, who, in confequence of being bound down to a fyftem
they do not approve, and having no fupport except that which they derive from
conforming to it, find themfelves under
the hard neceffity of either *prevaricating*
or *ftarving ?*———No one doubts but that
the Englifh clergy in general could with
more truth declare that they *do not,* than
that they *do* give their *unfeigned affent to*
all

all and every thing contained in the thirty-
nine Articles and the Book of Common-
Prayer ; and yet, with a folemn declaration
to this purpofe, are they obliged to enter
upon an office which above all offices requires thofe who exercife it to be examples
of fimplicity and fincerity.—Who can
help execrating the caufe of fuch an evil ?

But what I wifh moft to urge is the tendency of religious eftablifhments to im-
pede the improvement of the world. They
are boundaries prefcribed by human folly
to human inveftigation ; and inclofures
which intercept the light and confine the
exertions of reafon. Let any one imagine
to himfelf what effects fimilar eftablifhments would have in Philofophy, Navigation, Metaphyficks, Medicine or Mathe-
maticks. Something like this took place
in Logick and Philofophy; while the
IPSE DIXIT of Ariftotle and the nonfenfe
of the fchools maintained an authority like
that of the creeds of churchmen : And the
effect was a longer continuance of the
world in the ignorance and barbarity of
the dark ages. But civil eftablifhments of
religion are *more* pernicious. So apt are
mankind to mifreprefent the character of
the

the Deity, and to connect his favour with particular modes of faith, that it muft be expected, that a religion fo fettled will be what it has hitherto been — a gloomy and cruel fuperftition bearing the name of religion.

It has been long a fubject of difpute, which is worft in its effects on fociety, *fuch* a religion or fpeculative Atheifm. For my own part, I could almoft give the preference to the latter.——Atheism is fo repugnant to every principle of common fenfe, that it is not poffible it fhould ever gain much ground, or become very prevalent. On the contrary ; there is a particular pronenefs in the human mind to Superstition, and nothing is more likely to become prevalent.——Atheism leaves us to the full influence of moft of our natural feelings and focial principles; and thefe are fo ftrong in their operation, that in general they are a fufficient guard to the order of fociety. But Superstition counteracts thefe principles, by holding forth men to one another as objects of divine hatred ; and by putting them on harraffing, filencing, imprifoning and burning one another in order to do God fervice.——Atheism is a fanctuary for

vice

vice by taking away the motives to virtue arifing from the will of God and the fear of a future judgment. But SUPERSTITION is more a fanctuary for vice, by teaching men ways of pleafing God without moral virtue, and by leading them even to compound for wickednefs by *ritual* fervices, by bodily penances and mortifications, by adorning fhrines, going pilgrimages, faying many prayers, receiving abfolution from the prieft, exterminating heretics, &c.—ATHE-ISM deftroys the facrednefs and obligation of an oath. But has there not been alfo a religion (fo called) which has done this, by leading its profeffors to a perfuafion that there exifts a power on earth which can difpenfe with the obligation of oaths, that *pious* frauds are right, and that faith is not to be kept with heretics ?

It is indeed only a rational and liberal religion ; a religion founded on juft notions of the Deity as a being who regards equally every fincere worfhipper, and by whom all are alike favoured as far as they act up to the light they enjoy ; a religion which confifts in the imitation of the moral perfections of an almighty but benevolent governor of nature, who directs for the
beft

beft all events, in confidence in the care
of his providence, in refignation to his
will, and in the faithful difcharge of every
duty of piety and morality from a regard
to his authority and the apprehenfion of a
future righteous retribution.——It is only
THIS religion (the infpiring principle of
every thing fair and worthy and joyful,
and which in truth is nothing but the
love of God and man and virtue warming
the heart and directing the conduct.)—It is
only THIS kind of religion that can blefs
the world, or be an advantage to fociety.—
This is the religion that every enlightened
friend to mankind will be zealous to promote. But it is a religion that the powers
of the world know little of, and which
will always be beft promoted by being
left free and open.

I cannot help adding here, that fuch
in particular is the *Chriftian* religion.——
Chriftianity teaches us that there is none
good but one, that is, God ; that he willeth
all men to be faved, and will punifh nothing
but wickednefs ; that he defires mercy
and not facrifice (benevolence rather than
rituals) ; that loving him with all our hearts,
and loving our neighbour as ourfelves, is
the whole of our duty ; and that in every

nation

nation he that feareth him and worketh righteoufnefs is accepted of him. It refts its authority on the power of God, not of man ; refers itfelf entirely to the underftandings of men ; makes us the fubjects of a kingdom that is not of this world; and requires us to elevate our minds above temporal emoluments, and to look forwards to a ftate beyond the grave, where a government of perfect virtue will be erected under that Meffiah who has *tafted death for every man.*—What have the powers of the world to do with fuch a religion ?—It difclaims all connexion with them; it made its way at firft in oppofition to them; and, as far as it is now upheld by them, it is difhonoured and vilified.

The injury which civil eftablifhments do to Chriftianity may be learnt from the following confiderations.

Firft. The fpirit of religious eftablifhments is oppofite to the fpirit of Chriftianity. It is a fpirit of pride and tyranny in oppofition to the Chriftian *lowly* fpirit ; a contracted and felfifh fpirit, in oppofition to the Chriftian enlarged and benevolent fpirit; the fpirit of the world in oppofition to the Chriftian *heavenly* fpirit.

G　　　　　Secondly.

Secondly. Religious eſtabliſhments are founded on a claim of authority in the Chriſtian church which overthrows Chriſt's authority. He has in the ſcriptures given his followers a code of laws, to which he requires them to adhere as their *only* guide, But the language of the framers of church eſtabliſhments is—We *have authority in con-* " *troverſies of faith, and power to decree rites* " *and ceremonies.* We are the deputies of " Chriſt upon earth, who have been com- " miſſioned by him to interpret his laws, " and to rule his church. You muſt there- " fore follow US. The ſcriptures are inſuf- " ficient. Our interpretations you muſt " receive as Chriſt's laws ; our creeds as " *his* doctrine ; our inventions as *his* in- " ſtitutions."

It is evident, as the excellent HOADLY has ſhewn, that theſe claims turn Chriſt out of the government of his own king-dom, and place uſurpers on his throne.—— They are therefore derogatory to his ho-nour ; and a ſubmiſſion to them is a breach of the allegiance due to him. They have been almoſt fatal to true Chriſtianity ; and attempts to enforce them by civil penalties, have

have watered the Chriftian world with the blood of faints and martyrs.

Thirdly. The difficulty of introducing alterations into church eftablifhments after they have been once formed, is another objection to them. Hence it happens, that they remain always the fame amidft all changes of public manners and opinions * ; and that a kingdom even of Chriftans may go on for ages in idolatrous worfhip, after a general conviction may have taken place, that there is but *one* being who is the proper object of religious adoration, and that this *one* being is that one only living and true God who fent Chrift into the world, and who is *his* no lefs than he is *our* God and father. What a fad fcene of religious hypocrify muft fuch a difcordance between public conviction and the public forms pro-duce ?

* This is an inconvenience attending *civil* as well as *ecclefiaftical* eftablifhments, which has been with great wifdom guarded againft in the new *American* conftitu-tions, by appointing that there fhall be a revifal of them at the end of certain terms. This will leave them always open to improvement, without any danger of thofe convulfions which have ufually attended the cor-rections of abufes when they have acquired a facrednefs by time.

At

At this day, in fome *European* countries, the abfurdity and flavifhnefs of their hierarchies are feen and acknowledged ; but being incorporated with the ftate, it is fcarcely poffible to get rid of them.

What can be more ftriking than the State of *England* in this refpect ?—The fyftem of faith and worfhip eftablifhed in it was formed above two hundred years ago, when *Europe* was juft emerging from darknefs and barbarity. The times have ever fince been growing more enlightened ; but without any effect on the eftablifhment. Not a ray of the increafing light has penetrated it. Not one imperfection, however grofs, has been removed. The fame articles of faith are fubfcribed. The fame ritual of devotion is practifed.—There is reafon to fear that the *abfolution of the fick*, which forms a part of this ritual, is often reforted to as a paffport to heaven after a wicked life; and yet it is continued.—Perhaps nothing more fhocking to reafon and humanity ever made a part of a religious fyftem than the damning claufes in the *Athanafian* creed ; and yet the obligation of the clergy to declare affent to this creed, and to read it as a part of the public devotion, remains.

The

The neceffary confequence of fuch a ftate of things is, that,

Fourthly, Chriftianity itfelf is difgraced, and that all religion comes to be confidered as a ftate trick, and a barbarous mummery. It is well known, that in fome Popifh countries there are few Chriftians among the higher ranks of men, the religion of the State being in thofe countries *miftaken* for the religion of the Gofpel. This indeed fhews a criminal inattention in thofe who fall into fuch a miftake; for they ought to confider that Chriftianity has been grievoufly corrupted, and that their ideas of it fhould be taken from the New Teftament only. It is, however, fo natural to reckon Chriftianity to be that which it is held out to be in all the eftablifhments of it, that it cannot but happen that fuch an error will take place and produce fome of the worft confequences.——There is probably a greater number of rational Chriftians (that is, of Chriftians upon enquiry) in *England*, than in all Popifh countries. The reafon is, that the religious eftablifhment here is Popery *reformed*; and that a confiderable body diffent from it, and are often inculcating the neceffity of diftin-

guifhing

guifhing between the Chriftianity eftablifhed by law and that which is taught in the
Bible.——Certain it is, that till this diftinction is made, Chriftianity can never
recover its juft credit and ufefulnefs.

Such then are the effects of civil eftablifhments of religion. May heaven foon
put an end to them. The world will
never be generally wife or virtuous or
happy, till thefe enemies to its peace and
improvement are demolifhed. Thanks be
to God, they are giving way before increafing light. Let them never fhew themfelves in America. Let no fuch monfter
be known there as HUMAN AUTHORITY
IN MATTERS OF RELIGION. Let every
honeft and peaceable man, whatever is
his faith, be protected there ; and find an
effectual defence againft the attacks of bigotry and intolerance.—In the united States
may RELIGION flourifh. They cannot be
very great and happy if it does not. But let
it be a better religion than moft of thofe
which have been hitherto profeffed in the
world. Let it be a religion which enforces
moral obligations ; not a religion which re-
laxes and evades them.—A tolerant and *Ca-*
tholic

tholic religion; not a rage for profelitifm.—
A religion of peace and charity; not a
religion that perfecutes, curfes and damns.
——In a word, let it be the genuine Gofpel of peace lifting above the world, warming the heart with the love of God and
his creatures, and fuftaining the fortitude
of good men by the affured hope of a
future deliverance from death, and an infinite reward in the *everlafting kingdom of
our Lord and Saviour.*

From the preceding obfervations it may
be concluded, that it is impoffible I fhould
not admire the following article in the declaration of rights which forms the foundation of the *Maffachufett's* conftitution.—
" In this State every denomination of
" Chriftians demeaning themfelves peace-
" ably and as good fubjects of the com-
" monwealth, fhall be EQUALLY under the
" protection of the law; and no fubordi-
" nation of any one fect or denomination
" to another fhall ever be eftablifhed by
" law *."

* The *North Carolina* conftitution alfo orders that
there fhall be no eftablifhment of any one religious church
or denomination in that State in preference to any other.

I   This

This is liberal beyond all example. — I
fhould, however, have admired it more
had it been MORE liberal, and the words
ALL MEN OF ALL RELIGIONS been fubftituted for the words *every denomination
of Chriftians.*

It appears farther from the preceding
obfervations, that I cannot but diflike the
religious tefts which make a part of feveral
of the *American* conftitutions.———In the
Maffachufett's conftitution it is ordered, that
all who take feats in the Houfe of Reprefentatives or Senate fhall declare " their
" firm perfuafion of the truth of the
" Chriftian religion." The fame is required by the *Maryland* conftitution, as a
condition of being admitted into *any* places
of profit or truft. In *Penfylvania* every
member of the Houfe of Reprefentatives
is required to declare, that he " acknow-
" ledges the Scriptures of the Old and
" New Teftament to be given by divine
" infpiration." In the State of *Delaware,*
that " he believes in God the Father, and
" in Jefus Chrift his only Son, and in the
" Holy Ghoft, one God bleffed for ever-
" more." All this is more than is required even in *England,* where, though
every

every perfon however debauched or athe-
iftical is required to receive the facrament
as a qualification for *inferior* places, no
other religious teft is impofed on members of
parliament than a declaration againft Popery.
—It is an obfervation no lefs juft than common, that fuch tefts exclude only *honeſt*
men. The *dis*honeft never feruple them.

MONTESQUIEU probably was not a
Chriftian. NEWTON and LOCKE were not
Trinitarians ; and therefore not *Chriſtians*
according to the commonly received ideas
of Chriftianity. Would the United States,
for this reafon, deny fuch men, were they
living, all places of truft and power among
them ?

H   *Of*

Of EDUCATION.

SUCH is the ſtate of things which I wiſh to take place in the united *American* States.—In order to introduce and perpetuate it, and at the ſame time to give it the greateſt effect on the improvement of the world, nothing is more neceſſary than the eſtabliſhment of a wiſe and liberal plan of EDUCATION. It is impoſſible properly to repreſent the importance of this. So much is left by the author of nature to depend on the turn given to the mind in early life, and the impreſſions then made, that I have often thought there may be a *ſecret* remaining to be diſcovered in education, which will cauſe future generations to grow up virtuous and happy, and accelerate human improvement to a greater degree than can at preſent be imagined.

The end of education is to direct the powers of the mind in unfolding themſelves; and to aſſiſt them in gaining their juſt bent and force. And, in order to this,

its

its bufinefs fhould be to teach *how* to think, rather than *what* to think; or to lead into the beft way of fearching for truth, rather than to inftruct in truth itfelf.—As for the latter, who is qualified for it?—There are many indeed who are eager to undertake this office. All parties and fects think they have difcovered truth, and are confident that they alone are its advocates and friends. But the very different and inconfiftent accounts they give of it demonftrate they are utter ftrangers to it; and that it is better to teach *nothing*, than to teach what they hold out for truth. The greater their confidence, the greater is the reafon for diftrufting them. We generally fee the warmeft zeal, where the object of it is the greateft nonfenfe.

Such obfervations have a particular tendency to fhew that education ought to be an initiation into candour, rather than into any fyftems of faith; and that it fhould form a habit of cool and patient inveftigation, rather than an attachment to any opinions.

But hitherto education has been conducted on a contrary plan. It has been a *contraction*, not an *enlargement* of the

in-

intellectual faculties; an *injection* of falfe principles hardening them in error, not a *difcipline* enlightening and improving them. Inftead of opening and ftrengthening them, and teaching to think *freely*; it hath cramped and enflaved them, and qualified for thinking only in *one* track. Inftead of inftilling humility, charity, and liberality, and thus preparing for an eafier difcovery and a readier admiffion of truth; it has inflated with conceit, and ftuffed the human mind with wretched prejudices.

The more has been learnt from *fuch* education, the more it becomes neceffary to *un*learn. The more has been taught in this way, of fo much the more muft the mind be emptied before true wifdom can enter —Such was education in the time of the firft teachers of chriftianity. By furnifhing with fkill in the arts of difputation and fophiftry, and producing an attachment to eftablifhed fyftems, it turned the minds of men from truth, and rendered them more determined to refift evidence and more capable of evading it. Hence it happened, that this heavenly inftruction, when firft

com-

communicated, was *to the Jews a stumbling block, and to the Greeks foolishness*; and that, in spite of *miracles themselves*, the persons who rejected it with most disdain, and who opposed it with most violence, were those who had been educated in colleges, and were best versed in the false learning of the times : And had it taught the true philosophy instead of the true religion, the effect would have been the same. The doctrine " that the sun stood still, and that " the earth moved round it," would have been reckoned no less absurd and incredible, than the doctrine of a *crucified Messiah*. And the men who would have treated such an instruction with most contempt, would have been the *wise and the prudent*; that is, the proud sophists and learned doctors of the times, who had studied the *Ptolemaick* system of the world, and learnt, by cycles and epicycles, to account for all the motions of the heavenly bodies.

In like manner, when the improvement of Logick in Mr. Locke's *Essay on the Human Understanding* was first published in *Britain*, the persons readiest to attend to it and to receive it were those who had

never

never been trained in colleges; and whofe minds, therefore, had never been perverted by an inftruction in the jargon of the fchools. To the deep profeffors of the time, it appeared (like the doctrine taught in his book on the Reafonablenefs of Chriftianity) to be a dangerous novelty and herefy; and the Univerfity of Ox-FORD, in particular, condemned and reprobated the author.——The like happened when Sir ISAAC NEWTON's difcoveries were firft publifhed. A romance (that is, the Philofophy of DESCARTES) was then in poffeffion of the philofophical world. Education had rivetted it in the minds of the learned; and it was twenty-feven years before NEWTON's *Principia* could gain fufficient credit to bring it to a fecond edition.—Such are the prejudices which have generally prevailed againft new lights. Such the impediments which have been thrown in the way of improvement by a narrow plan of education.—Even now the principal object of education (efpecially in divinity) is to teach eftablifhed fyftems as certain truths, and to qualify for fuccefs-fully defending them againft opponents; and

and thus to arm the mind againſt conviction, and render it impenetrable to farther
light. Indeed, were it offered to my option which I would have, the plain ſenſe
of a common and untutored man, or the
deep erudition of the proud ſcholars and
profeſſors in moſt univerſities, I ſhould
eagerly prefer the former, from a per-
ſuaſion that it would leave me at a leſs
diſtance from real wiſdom. An unoccupied
and ſimple mind is infinitely preferable
to a mind warped by ſyſtems; and the
entire *want* of learning better than a learning, ſuch as moſt of that is which hitherto
has been ſought and admired—A learning
which puffs up, while in reality it is nothing but profounder ignorance and more
inveterate prejudice.

It may be worth adding here, that a narrow education (ſhould it ever happen not
to produce the evils now mentioned) will
probably produce equal evils of a contrary
nature. I mean, that there will be danger,
when perſons ſo educated come to ſee the
abſurdity of *ſome* of the opinions in which
they have been educated, that they will
become prejudiced againſt them *all*, and,
conſequently, throw them *all* away, and
run

run wild into fcepticifm and infidelity. — At prefent, in this part of the world this is a very common event.

I am by no means qualified to give a juft account of the particular method in which education ought to be conducted, fo as to avoid thefe evils: That is, fo as to render the mind free and unfettered; quick in difcerning evidence, and prepared to follow it from whatever quarter and in whatever manner it may offer itfelf. But certain it is, that the beft mode of education is that which does this moft effectually; which guards beft againft filly prejudices; which enflames moft with the love of truth; which difpofes moft to ingenuity and fairnefs; and leaves the mind moft fenfible of its own need of farther information. — Had this been always the aim of education, mankind would now have been farther advanced. — It fuppofes, however, an *improved* ftate of mankind; and when once it has taken place, it will quicken the progrefs of *im-provement*.

I have in thefe obfervations expreffed a diflike of fyftems; but I have meant only

to

to condemn that attachment to them as ftandards of truth which has been too prevalent. It may be neceffary in education to make ufe of them ; or of books explaining them. But they fhould be ufed only as guides and helps to enquiry. Inftruction in them fhould be attended with a fair exhibition of the evidence on both fides of every queftion ; and care fhould be taken to induce, as far as poffible, a habit of believing only on an overbalance of evidence ; and of proportioning affent in every cafe to the degree of that overbalance, without regarding authority, antiquity, fingularity, novelty, or any of the prejudices which too commonly influence affent.——Nothing is fo well fitted to produce this habit as the ftudy of *mathematics*. In thefe fciences no one ever thinks of giving his affent to a propofition till he can clearly underftand it, and fee it proved by a fair deduction from propofitions previoufly underftood and proved. In thefe fciences the mind is inured to clofe and patient attention ; fhewn the nature of juft reafoning ; and taught to form diftinct ideas, and to expect clear evidence in all cafes before belief. They furnifh, therefore, the beft exercife for the intellec-

I   tual

tual powers, and the beſt defence againſt that credulity and precipitation and confuſion of ideas which are the common ſources of error.

There is, however, a danger even here to be avoided. Mathematical ſtudies may abſorb the attention too much; and when they do, they contract the mind by rendering it incapable of thinking *at large*; by diſqualifying it for judging of any evidence except mathematical; and, conſequently, diſpoſing it to an unreaſonable ſcepticiſm on all ſubjects which admit not of ſuch evidence.——There have been many inſtances of this narrowneſs in mathematicians.

But to return from this digreſſion, — I cannot help obſerving on this occaſion, with reſpect to CHRISTIANITY in particular, that education ought to lead to a habit of judging of it as it is in the code itſelf of Chriſtianity; that the doctrines it reveals ſhould be learnt only from a critical and fair enquiry into the ſenſe of this code; and that all inſtruction in it ſhould be a preparation for making this enquiry and a communication of aſſiſtance in examining into the proofs of its divine original, and in determining to what degree of

evidence

evidence thefe proofs amount, after allowing every difficulty its juft weight. ——
This has never yet been the practice among
Chriftians. The New Teftament has been
reckoned hitherto an *infufficient* ftandard of
Chriftian Divinity ; and, therefore, formularies of human invention *pretending* to
explain and define it (but in reality mifre-
prefenting and difhonouring it) have been
fubftituted in its room ; and teaching *thefe*
has been called teaching *Chriftianity*. And
it is very remarkable, that in the *Englifh*
Univerfities Lectures on the New Teftament are feldom or ever read; and that,
through all Chriftendom, it is much lefs an
object of attention than the *fyftems* and *creeds*
which have been fathered upon it.

I will only add on this fubject, that it is
above all things neceffary, while inftruction
is conveyed, to convey with it a fenfe of
the imbecility of the human mind, and of
its great pronenefs to error ; and alfo a
difpofition, even on points which feem the
moft clear, to liften to objections, and to
confider nothing as involving in it our final
intereft but an HONEST HEART.

Nature

Nature has fo made us, that an attachment muſt take place within us to opinions
once formed; and it was proper that we
ſhould be fo made, in order to prevent that
levity and defultorineſs of mind which muſt
have been the confequence had we been
ready to give up our opinions too eaſily and
haſtily. But this natural tendency, however wiſely given us, is apt to exceed its
proper limits, and to render us unreaſon-
ably tenacious. It ought, therefore, like
all our other natural propenſities, to be
carefully watched and guarded; and education ſhould put us upon doing this. An
obſervation before made ſhould, in particular, be inculcated, " that all mankind
" have hitherto been moſt tenacious when
" moſt in the wrong, and reckoned them-
" felves moſt enlightened when moſt in the
" dark."———This is, indeed, a very morti-
fying fact; but attention to it is neceſſary
to cure that miſerable pride and dogmati-
calneſs which are fome of the worſt enemies to improvement. —— Who is there
that does not remember the time when he
was entirely ſatisfied about points which
deeper reflexion has ſhewn to be above his
comprehenſion? Who, for inſtance, does

not

not remember a time when he would have
wondered at the queftion, " why does
" water run down hill ?" What ignorant man is there who is not perfuaded
that he underftands this perfectly ? But
every *improved* man knows it to be a queftion he cannot anfwer ; and what diftin-
guifhes him in this inftance from the lefs
improved part of mankind is his know-
ing this. The like is true in numberlefs
other inftances. One of the beft proofs of
wifdom is a fenfe of our want of wifdom ;
and he who knows moft poffeffes moft of
this fenfe.

In thinking of myfelf I derive fome encouragement from this reflexion. I now
fee, that I do not underftand many points
which once appeared to me very clear.
The more I have inquired, the more fenfible I have been growing of my own darknefs ; and a part of the hiftory of my life
is that which follows.

In early life I was ftruck with Bifhop
BUTLER's *Analogy of religion natural and
revealed to the conftitution and courfe of nature.* I reckon it happy for me that this

book

book was one of the firft that fell into my hands. It taught me the proper mode of reafoning on moral and religious fub-jects, and particularly the importance of paying a due regard to the imperfection of human knowledge. His Sermons alfo, I then thought, and do ftill think, excellent. Next to *his* works, I have always been an admirer of the writings of Dr. CLARK. And I cannot help adding, however ftrange it may feem, that I owe much to the phi-lofophical writings of Mr. HUME, which I likewife ftudied early in life. Though an enemy to his Scepticifm, I have profited by it. By attacking, with great ability, every principle of truth and reafon, he put me upon examining the ground upon which I ftood, and taught me not haftily to take any thing for granted.——The firft fruits of my reading and ftudies were laid before the public in a Treatife entitled *A* REVIEW *of the principal Queftions and Diffi-culties in Morals.* This publication has been followed by many others on various fubjects.—And now, in the evening of a life devoted to enquiry and fpent in en-deavours (weak indeed and feeble) to ferve

the

the beft interefts, prefent and future, of mankind, I am waiting for the GREAT TEACHER, convinced that the order of nature is perfect; that infinite wifdom and goodnefs govern all things; and that Chriftianity comes from God : But at the fame time puzzled by many difficulties, anxious for more light, and refting with full and conftant affurance only on this ONE truth —— That the practice of virtue is the duty and dignity of man; and, in all events, his wifeft and fafeft courfe.

Of the DANGERS *to which the* American *States are expofed.*

IN the preceding obfervations, I have aimed at pointing out the means of promoting the progrefs of improvement in the united States of America. I have infifted, particularly, on the importance of a juft fettlement of the FEDERAL UNION, and the eftablifhment of a well-guarded and perfect liberty in fpeculation, in government, in education, and in religion.——— The united States are now fetting out, and all depends on the care and forefight with which a plan is begun, which hereafter will require only to be ftrengthened and ripened. This is, therefore, the time for giving them advice; and mean advice (like the prefent) may fuggeft fome ufeful hints. ——— In this country, when any improvements are propofed, or any corrections are attempted of abufes fo grofs as to make our boafts of liberty ridiculous *, a

clamour

---

* The majority of the BRITISH Houfe of Commons is chofen by a *few thoufands* of the dregs of the people, who are conftantly paid for their votes.———

Is

clamour immediately arifes againft INNO-
VATION; and an alarm fpreads, left the attempt to *repair* fhould *deftroy.*——In America no fuch prejudices can operate. *There*
abufes have not yet gained facrednefs by
time. *There* the way is open to focial dignity and happinefs; and reafon may utter
her voice with confidence and fuccefs.

Is it not *ridiculous* to call a country *fo* governed *free ?*
—— See a ftriking account of the State of the Britifh
Parliamentary Reprefentation, in Mr. *Burgh's* Political
Difquifitions, Vol. I. p. 39, &c.

It was propofed to the convention for fettling the *Maffachufett's* conftitution, that *one* of the two houfes which
conftitute the *general court* of that State fhould be a reprefentation of *perfons,* and the *other* a reprefentation of *property;* and that the body of the people fhould appoint
only the *electors* of their reprefentatives.—By fuch regulations corruption in the choice of reprefentatives
would be rendered lefs practicable; and it feems the
beft method of concentering in the Legiflature as much
as poffible of the virtue and ability of the State, and of
making its voice always an expreffion of the will and
beft fenfe of the people.—On this plan alfo, the number
of members conftituting a Legiflature might be much
leffened.—This is a circumftance of particular confequence, to which the united States, in fome future period
of their increafe, will find it neceffary to attend. It has
been often juftly obferved, that a legiflative body very
numerous is little better than a *mob.*

K   *Of*

Of DEBTS *and* INTERNAL WARS.

I HAVE obferved in the introduction to this Addrefs, that the *American* States have many dangers to fhun. In what follows I fhall give a brief recital of fome of the chief of thefe dangers.

The danger from an endlefs increafe of PUBLIC DEBTS has been already fufficiently noticed.

Particular notice has been likewife taken of the danger from INTERNAL WARS.— Again and again, I would urge the neceffity of purfuing every meafure and ufing every precaution which can guard againft this danger. It will be fhocking to fee in the *new* world a repetition of all the evils which have hitherto laid wafte the *old* world —War raging where peace and liberty were thought to have taken their abodes — The points of bayonets and the mouths of cannon fettling difputes, inftead of the collected wifdom of the confederation — and perhaps one reftlefs and ambitious State rifing by bloody

bloody conqueſt above the reſt, and becoming a *ſovereign* State, claiming impiouſly (as *Britain* once did) " full authority to make " laws that ſhall bind its ſiſter States in all " caſes whatever," and drawing to itſelf all advantages at their expence.——I deprecate this calamity. I ſhudder when I conſider how poſſible it is ; and hope thoſe perſons are miſtaken who think that ſuch are the jealouſies which govern human nature, and ſuch the imperfections of the beſt human arrangements, that it is not within the reach of any wiſdom to diſcover any effectual means of preventing it, without encroaching too much on the liberty and independence of the States. I have mentioned an enlargement of the powers of CONGRESS. Others have propoſed a conſolidation of the powers of government in one PARLIAMENT repreſenting *all* the States, and ſuperſeding the particular parliaments by which they are now ſeparately governed. But it is obvious, that this will be attended with greater inconveniencies, and encroach more on the liberty of the States, than the enlargement I have propoſed of the powers of CONGRESS. ——- If

K 2   ſuch

ſuch a parliament is not to ſuperſede any of the other parliaments, it will be the ſame with CONGRESS as at preſent conſtituted.

Of an UNEQUAL DISTRIBUTION OF PROPERTY.

IT is a trite obſervation, that " dominion " is founded on property." Moſt free States have manifeſted their ſenſe of the truth of this obſervation, by ſtudying to find out means of preventing too great an inequality in the diſtribution of property. What tumults were occaſioned at ROME, in its beſt times, by attempts to carry into execution the *Agrarian* law ? Among the people of *Iſrael,* by the direction of heaven, all eſtates which had been alienated during the courſe of fifty years, returned to their original owners at the end of that term. One of the circumſtances that has been moſt favourable to the *American* States in forming their new conſtitutions of government has been the equality which ſubſiſts among them.

The

The happieſt ſtate of man is the middle
ſtate between the *ſavage* and the *refined,* or
between the wild and the luxurious ſtate.
Such is the ſtate of ſociety in CONNEC-
TICUT, and ſome others of the *American*
provinces ; where the inhabitants conſiſt, if
I am rightly informed, of an independent
and hardy YEOMANRY, all nearly on a
level—trained to arms,—inſtructed in their
rights—cloathed in home-ſpun—of ſimple
manners — ſtrangers to luxury — drawing
plenty from the ground—and that plenty,
gathered eaſily by the hand of induſtry;
and giving riſe to early marriages, a numerous progeny, length of days, and a rapid
increaſe—the rich and the poor, the haughty
grandee and the creeping ſycophant, equally
unknown—protected by laws, which (being their own will) cannot oppreſs; and
by an equal government, which wanting
lucrative places, cannot create corrupt can-
vaſſings * and ambitious intrigue.——O diſtinguiſhed people ! May you continue

---

* In this State, and alſo the State of *Maſſachuſetts,*
New Jerſey, &c. any attempt to canvas, or even the ex-
preſſion of a wiſh to be choſen, will exclude a candi-
date from a ſeat in the Houſe of Repreſentatives. The
ſame is true of any ſtain on his moral character.

long

long thus happy; and may the happinefs
you enjoy fpread over the face of the whole
earth !—But I am forgetting myfelf. There
is danger that a ftate of fociety fo happy will
not be of long duration ; that fimplicity and
virtue will give way to depravity ; that equality will in time be loft, the curfed luft of do-
mineering fhew itfelf, liberty languifh, and
civil government gradually degenerate into
an inftrument in the hands of the *few* to
opprefs and plunder the *many*.—Such has
hitherto been the progrefs of evil in human
affairs. In order to give them a better
turn, fome great men (*Plato,* Sir *Thomas
More,* Mr. *Wallace,* &c.) have propofed
plans, which, by eftablifhing a community
of goods and annihilating property, would
make it impoffible for any one member of
a State to think of enflaving the reft, or
to confider himfelf as having any intereft
diftinct from that of his fellow-citizens.
Such theories are in fpeculation pleafing ;
nor perhaps are they wholly impracticable.
Some approaches to them may hereafter be
made ; and fchemes of government may take
place, which fhall leave fo little, befides
perfonal merit, to be a means of diftinction,

as

as to exclude from fociety moft of the caufes of evil. But be this as it will ; it is out of doubt that there is an equality in fociety which is effential to liberty, and which every State that would continue virtuous and happy ought as far as poffible to maintain. — It is not in my power to defcribe the beft method of doing this. — I will only obferve, that there are THREE enemies to equality againft which *America* ought to guard.

First; Granting hereditary honours and titles of nobility. Perfons thus diftinguifhed, though perhaps meaner than the meaneft of their dependents, are apt to confider themfelves as belonging to a higher order of beings, and *made* for power and government. Their birth and rank neceffarily difpofe them to be hoftile to general liberty; and when they are not fo, and difcover a juft zeal for the rights of mankind, it is always a triumph of good fenfe and virtue over the temptations of their fituation. It is, therefore, with peculiar fatisfaction that I have found in the articles of confederation an order that no titles of nobility fhall be ever granted by the united States. Let there

there be honours to encourage merit ; but
let them die with the men who have earned
them.   Let them not defcend to pofterity
to fofter a fpirit of domination, and to
produce a proud and tyrannical ariftocracy.
—In a word, let the united States continue
for ever what it is now their glory to be—a
confederation of States profperous and happy,
without Lords—without Bishops*—and
without Kings.

Secondly ; The right of primogeniture.
The tendency of this to produce an improper inequality is very obvious.   The
difpofition to raife a name, by accumulating property in one branch of a family,
is a vanity no lefs unjuft and cruel, than

* I do not mean by *Bifhops* any officers among Chriftians merely *fpiritual* ; but *Lords fpiritual*, as diftinguifhed from *Lords temporal*, or Clergymen raifed to pre-
eminence, and invefted with civil honours and authority,
by a State eftablifhment.

I muft add, that by what is here faid I do not mean
to exprefs a *general* preference of a *republican* conftitution
of government.   There is a degree of political degeneracy which unfits for fuch a conftitution.   Britain,
in particular, confifts too much of the high and the low,
(of *fcum* and *dregs*) to admit of it.   Nor will it fuit *America*, fhould it ever become equally corrupt.

3   dangerous

dangerous to the intereſt of liberty ; and no wiſe State will encourage or tolerate it.

Thirdly ; FOREIGN TRADE is another of the enemies againſt which I wiſh to caution the united States. But this operates unfavourably to a State in ſo many more ways than by deſtroying that equality which is the baſis of liberty, that it will be proper to take more particular notice of it.

Of

Of Trade, Banks, *and* Paper Credit.

FOREIGN trade has, in fome refpects, the moft ufeful tendency. By creating an intercourfe between diftant kingdoms, it extends benevolence, removes local prejudices, leads every man to confider himfelf more as a citizen of the world than of any particular State, and, confequently, checks the exceffes of that *Love of our Country* * which has been applauded as one

---

* The love of our country is then only a noble paffion when it engages us to promote the *internal* happinefs of our country, and to defend its rights and liberties againft domeftic and foreign invafion, maintaining at the fame time an equal regard to the rights and liberties of other countries. But this has not been its moft common effects. On the contrary, it has in general been nothing but a fpirit of rivalfhip between different communities, producing contention and a thirft for conqueft and dominion. — What is his *country* to a *Ruffian*, a *Turk*, a *Spaniard*, &c. but a fpot where he enjoys no right, and is difpofed of by owners as if he was a beaft? And what is his *love* to his country but an attachment to degradation and flavery?—What was the love of their country among the *Jews* but a wretched partiality for themfelves and a proud contempt for other nations? Among

one of the nobleſt, but which, *really*, is one of the moſt *deſtructive* principles in human nature. —— Trade alſo, by enabling every country to draw from other countries conveniencies and advantages which it cannot find within itſelf, produces among nations a ſenſe of mutual dependence, and promotes the general improvement. — But there is no part of mankind to which theſe uſes of trade are of leſs conſequence than the *American* States. They are ſpread over a great continent, and make a world within themſelves. The country they inhabit includes ſoils and climates of all ſorts, producing not only every *neceſſary*, but every *convenience* of life. And the vaſt rivers and wide-ſpread lakes which interſect it, create ſuch an inland communication between its different parts, as is unknown in any other region of the earth. They poſſeſs then within themſelves the

Among the *Romans* alſo what was it, however great in many of its exertions, but a principle holding together a band of robbers in their attempts to cruſh all liberty but their own ?—Chriſtianity has wiſely omitted to recommend this principle. Had it done this, it would have countenanced a vice among mankind.—It has done what is infinitely better — It has recommended UNIVERSAL BENEVOLENCE.

beſt

beſt means of the moſt profitable traffic, and the ampleſt ſcope for it. Why ſhould they look much farther? What occaſion have they for being anxious about puſhing *foreign* trade; or even about raiſing a great naval force? — Britain, indeed, conſiſting as it does of *unarmed* inhabitants, and threatened as it is by ambitious and powerful neighbours, cannot hope to maintain its exiſtence long after becoming open to invaſion by loſing its naval ſuperiority. —— But this is not the caſe with the American States. They have no powerful neighbours to dread. The vaſt Atlantic muſt be croſſed before they can be attacked. They are all a well-trained *militia*; and the ſucceſsful reſiſtance which, in their infancy and without a naval force, they have made to the invaſion of the firſt *European* power, will probably diſcourage and prevent all future invaſions. Thus ſingularly happy, why ſhould they ſeek connexions with *Europe,* and expoſe themſelves to the danger of being involved in its quarrels? — What have they to do with its politics? — Is there any thing very important to them which they can draw from thence—except INFECTION?——Indeed,

deed, I tremble when I think of that rage for trade which is likely to prevail among them. It may do them infinite mifchief. All nations are fpreading fnares for them, and courting them to a dangerous intercourfe. Their beft intereft requires them to guard themfelves by all proper means ; and, particularly, by laying heavy duties on importations. But in no cafe will any means fucceed unlefs aided by MANNERS. In this inftance, particularly, there is reafon to fear that an increafing paffion for foreign frippery will render all the beft regulations ineffectual. And fhould this happen, that fimplicity of character, that manlinefs of fpirit, that difdain of tinfel in which true dignity confifts, will difappear. Effeminacy, fervility and venality will enter ; and liberty and virtue be fwallowed up in the gulph of corruption. Such may be the courfe of events in the American States. Better *infinitely* will it be for them to confift of bodies of plain and honeft farmers, than of opulent and fplendid merchants. —— Where in thefe States do the pureft manners prevail ? Where do the inhabitants live moft on an equality, and moft at their eafe ? Is

it

it not in thofe inland parts where agriculture gives health and plenty, and trade
is fcarcely known ?——Where, on the contrary, are the inhabitants moſt felfiſh, luxurious, loofe, and vicious; and at the fame
time moſt unhappy ? Is it not along the
fea coaſts, and in the great towns, where
trade flouriſhes and merchants abound ?——
So ſtriking is the effect of thefe different
fituations on the vigour and happinefs of
human life, that in the one population
would languiſh did it receive no aid from
emigrations; while in the other it increafes
to a degree fcarcely ever before known.

But to proceed to fome obfervations of a
different nature——

The united States have, I think, particular reafon to dread the following effects of
foreign trade.

By increafing importation to feed luxury
and gratify prodigality, it will carry out
their coin, and occafion the fubſtitution of a
delufive paper currency; the confequence
of which will be, that *ideal* wealth will
take place of *real*, and their fecurity come
to depend on the ſtrength and duration of a
Bubble. ——I am very fenfible that paper
credit

credit is one of the greateſt of all conveniencies ; but this makes it likewiſe one of
the greateſt of all temptations. A public
Bank, (while it can circulate its bills) faci-
litates commerce, and aſſiſts the exertions
of a State in proportion to its credit. But
when it is not carefully reſtricted and
watched ; when its emiſſions exceed the
coin it can command, and are carried near
the utmoſt length that the confidence of
the public will allow ; and when, in conſequence of this, its permanence comes to
depend on the permanence of public credulity — In theſe circumſtances, a BANK,
though it may for a time (that is, while a
balance of trade too unfavourable does
not occaſion a run, and no events ariſe
which produce alarm) anſwer all the ends
of a MINE from which millions may be
drawn in a minute ; and, by filling a kingdom with caſh, render it capable of ſuſ-
taining *any* debts, and give it a kind of
OMNIPOTENCE. — In ſuch circumſtances,
I ſay, notwithſtanding theſe temporary advantages, a public BANK muſt *at laſt* prove
a great calamity ; and a kingdom ſo ſup-
ported, at the very time of its greateſt

exer-

exertions, will be only ftriving more violently to increafe the horror of an approching convulfion.

The united States have already verified fome of thefe obfervations, and felt in fome degree the confequences to which I have alluded. They have been carried through the war by an emiffion of paper which had no folid fupport, and which now has loft all value. It is indeed furprifing that, being fecured on no fund and incapable of being exchanged for coin, it fhould ever have obtained a currency, or anfwered any important purpofe.

Unhappily for *Britain*, it has ufed the means of giving more ftability to its paper-credit, and been enabled by it to fupport expences greater than any that have been yet known, and to contract a debt which now *aftonifhes*, and may hereafter produce a cataftrophe that will *terrify* the world.— A longer duration of the late war would have brought on this cataftrophe immediately. The PEACE has put it off *for the prefent*. God grant, if ftill poffible, that meafures may be adopted which fhall put it off *for ever*.

Of

Of O A T H S.

OATHS are expedients to which all States have had recourfe in order to obtain true information and afcertain facts by fecuring the veracity of witneffes. But I know not how to relifh that *imprecation* which always makes a part of an oath. Perhaps, there is no fuch neceffity for it as is commonly imagined. An AFFIR-MATION folemnly made, with laws in-flicting fevere penalties on falfhood when detected, would probably anfwer all the ends of oaths.—I am, therefore, difpofed to wifh, that in the united States *impre-catory* oaths may be abolifhed, and the fame indulgence in this refpect granted to all which is now granted to the *Quakers.* But I am afraid they will think this too dangerous an experiment ; and what is of moft confequence is to avoid,

Firft, Such a multiplicity of oaths as will render them too familiar.

And, Secondly, A flight manner of ad-miniftering them. ENGLAND, in this re-

M   fpect.

spect, seems to be sunk to the lowest possible degree of degeneracy. Oaths among us are required on so many occasions, and so carelessly administered, as to have lost almost all their use and efficacy. It has been asserted, that, including oaths of office, oaths at elections, custom-house oaths, &c. &c. there are about a *million* of perjuries committed in this kingdom *annually*. —— This is one of the most atrocious of our national iniquities ; and it is a wonder if we are not to be visited for it with some of the severest of God's judgments.

Of

Of the Negro Trade and Slavery.

THE Negro Trade cannot be cen-
sured in language too severe. It is a
traffick which, as it has been hitherto carried on, is shocking to humanity, cruel,
wicked, and diabolical. I am happy to
find that the united States are entering into
measures for discountenancing it, and for
abolishing the odious slavery which it has
introduced. 'Till they have done this, it
will not appear they deserve the liberty
for which they have been contending. For
it is self-evident, that if there are any men
whom they have a right to hold in slavery,
there may be *others* who have had a right
to hold *them* in slavery. * —— I am sensible,
however, that this is a work which they
cannot accomplish at once. The emanci-
pation of the Negroes must, I suppose, be
left in some measure to be the effect of

* See a remonstrance, full of energy, directed to the
united States on this Subject, by a very warm and able
friend to the rights of mankind, in a Tract, entitled—
Fragment of an original Letter on the Slavery of the Negroes;
written in the year 1776, but published in 1784, by
Thomas Day, Esq.

time

time and of manners. But nothing can excufe the united States if it is not done with as much fpeed, and at the fame time with as much effect, as their particular circumftances and fituation will allow. I rejoice that on this occafion I can recommend to them the example of my own country.——In *Britain*, a *Negro* becomes a *freeman* the moment he fets his foot on *Britifh* ground.

Conclusion.

SUCH is the advice which I would *humbly* (but *earneftly*) offer to the united States of *America*. —— Such are the means by which they may become the feats of liberty, fcience, peace, and virtue; happy within themfelves, and a refuge to the world.

Often, while employed in writing thefe papers, have I wifhed for a warning voice of more power. The prefent moment, however aufpicious to the united States if wifely improved, is critical ; and, though apparently the end of all their dangers, may

prove

prove the time of their greateſt danger.
I have, indeed, ſince finiſhing this Addreſs, been mortified more than I can ex-
preſs by accounts which have led me
to fear that I have carried my ideas of
them too high, and deceived myſelf with
viſionary expectations.——And ſhould this
be true — Should the return of peace and
the pride of independence lead them to
ſecurity and diſſipation — Should they loſe
thoſe virtuous and ſimple manners by
which alone Republics can long ſubſiſt—
Should falſe refinement, luxury, and irre-
ligion ſpread among them ; exceſſive jea-
louſy diſtract their governments ; and
claſhing intereſts, ſubject to no ſtrong
controul, break the federal union——The
conſequence will be, that the faireſt experiment ever tried in human affairs will
miſcarry ; and that a REVOLUTION which
had revived the hopes of good men and
promiſed an opening to better times, will
become a diſcouragement to all future efforts in favour of liberty, and prove only
an opening to a new ſcene of human degeneracy and miſery.

A DV E R-

ADVERTISEMENT.

THE following letter was written by the late M. *Turgot*, Comptroller General (in the years 1774, 1775, and 1776) of the finances of FRANCE. It contains obfervations in which the United States are deeply concerned; and, for this reafon, I now convey it to them, not doubting but that the eminence of M. *Turgot's* name and character will recommend it to their attention, and that it will do honour to his memory among all the friends of public liberty.

A Monfieur

A Monſieur P R I C E,

A Londres.

A Paris, le 22 Mars, 1778.

MR. FRANKLIN m'a remis, Monſieur, de votre part, la nouvelle édition de vos obſervations ſur la liberté civile, &c. Je vous dois un double remerciment ; 1° de votre ouvrage dont je connois depuis longtems le prix, et que j'avois lu avec avidité, malgré les occupations multipliées, dont j'etois aſ-failli, lorſqu'il a paru pour la premiere fois ; 2° de l'honnêteté que vous avez eue de re-trancher l'imputation de maladreſſe * que vous aviez mêlée au bien que vous diſiez d'ailleurs de moi dans vos obſervations addi-tionelles. J'aurois pu la meriter, ſi vous n'aviez eu en vue d'autre maladreſſe que celle de n'avoir pas ſçu demêler les reſſorts d'intrigues que faiſoient jouer contre moi des gens beaucoup plus *adroits* en ce genre que je ne le ſuis, que je ne le ſerai jamais, et que je ne veux l'etre. Mais il m'a paru que vous m'imputiez la maladreſſe d'avoir choqué groſſierement l'opinion générale de

---

* See the Notes annexed to the Tranſlation of this Letter.

ma

ma nation ; et à cet égard je crois que vous n'aviez rendu juſtice ni à moi, ni à ma nation, où il y a beaucoup plus de lumieres qu'on ne le croit généralement chez vous, et où peut-être il eſt plus aiſé que chez vous même de ramener le public à des idées raiſonnables. J'en juge par l'infatuation de votre nation ſur ce projet abſurde de ſubjuguer l'Amérique, qui a duré juſqu'à ce que l'aventure de Burgoyne ait commencé à lui deſſiller les yeux. J'en juge par le ſyſtême de monopole et d'excluſion qui règne chez tous vos écrivains politiques ſur le commerce, (J'excepte Mr. Adam Smith et le Doyen Tucker) ſyſtême qui eſt le véritable principe de votre ſéparation avec vos colonies. J'en juge par tous vos écrits polémiques ſur les queſtions qui vous agitent depuis une vingtaine d'années, et dans leſquels avant que le vôtre eut paru, je ne me rappelle preſque pas d'en avoir lu un, où le vrai point de la queſtion ait été ſaiſi. Je n'ai pas conçu comment une nation qui a cultivé avec tant de ſuccès toutes les branches des ſciences naturelles a pu reſter ſi fort au deſſous d'elle même, dans la ſcience la plus intereſſante de toutes, celle du bonheur public ; dans une ſcience où la liberté de la preſſe, dont elle ſeule jouit,

N   auroit

auroit dû lui donner fur toutes les autres
nations de l'Europe un avantage prodi-
gieux. Eſt-ce l'orgueil national qui vous a
empêchés de mettre à profit cet avantage?
Eſt-ce parce que vous etiez un peu moins
mal que les autres, que vous avez tourné
toutes vos ſpéculations à vous perſuader que
vous etiez bien ? Eſt-ce l'eſprit de parti, et
l'envie de ſe faire un appui des opinions
populaires qui a retardé vos progrès, en
portant vos politiques à traiter de vaine
métaphyſique toutes les ſpéculations qui
tendent à établir des principes fixes ſur
les droits et les vrais interêts des individus
et des nations ? Comment ſe fait-il que
vous ſoyez preſque le premier parmi vos
écrivains qui ayez donné des notions juſtes
de la liberté, et qui ayez fait ſentir la
fauſſeté de cette notion rebattue par preſque tous les écrivains les plus républicains,
que la liberté conſiſte à n'être ſoumis
qu'aux loix, comme ſi un homme opprimé
par une loi injuſte êtoit libre. Cela ne ſeroit
pas même vrai quand on ſuppoſeroit que
toutes les loix font l'ouvrage de la nation
aſſemblée ; car enfin l'individu a auſſi des
droits que la nation ne peut lui ôter, que
par la violence et par un uſage illegitime de
la force générale. Quoique vous ayez eu
égard

égard à cette verité, et que vous vous en foyez
expliqué, peut-être méritoit-elle que vous
la dévelopaffiez avec plus d'étendue, vû
le peu d'attention qu'y ont donnée même
les plus zelés partifans de la liberté.

C'eft encore une chofe étrange que ce ne
fût pas en Angleterre une vérité triviale de
dire qu'une nation ne peut jamais avoir
droit de gouverner une autre nation ; et
qu'un pareil gouvernement ne peut avoir
d'autre fondement que la force, qui eft auffi
le fondement du brigandage et de la tyrannie ; que la tyrannie d'un peuple eft de
toutes les tyrannies connues la plus cruelle
et la plus intolérable, celle qui laiffe le
moins de reffource à l'opprimé ; car enfin
un defpote eft arrêté par fon propre interêt,
il a le frein du remords, ou celui de l opinion publique, mais une multitude ne cal-
cule rien, n'a jamais de remords, et fe de-
cerne à elle même la gloire lors qu'elle
mérite le plus de honte.

Les événemens font pour la nation
Angloife un terrible commentaire de
votre livre. Depuis quelques mois ils
fe précipitent avec une rapidité très ac-
célérée.

celérée. Le dénouement eſt arrivé par rap-
port à l'Amérique. La voila indépendante
ſans retour. Sera-t'elle libre et heureuſe ?
Ce peuple nouveau ſitué ſi avantageuſe-
ment pour donner au monde l'exemple d'une
conſtitution où l'hommé jouiſſe de tous ſes
droits, exerce librement routes ſes facultés,
et ne ſoit gouverné que par la nature, la
raiſon et la juſtice, ſaura-t'il former une
pareille conſtitution ? ſaura-t'il l'affermir ſur
des fondemens éternels, prévenir toutes les
cauſes de diviſion et de corruption qui
peuvent la miner peu-à-peu et la détruire ?

Je ne ſuis point content je l'avoue des
conſtitutions qui ont été rédigées juſqu'à-
préſent par les différens Etats Américains.
Vous reprochez avec raiſon à celle de la
Penſylvanie le ſerment religieux exigé pour
avoir entrée dans le corps des repréſentans.
C'eſt bien pis dans les autres ; il y en a une,
je crois que c'eſt celle des Jerſeis qui exige
* *
Je vois dans le plus grand nombre l'imitation ſans objet des uſages de l'Angleterre.
Au lieu de ramener toutes les autorités à
une ſeule, celle de la nation, l'on établit des
corps différens, un corps des repréſentans,
un

un conſeil, un gouverneur, parce que l'Angleterre a une chambre des communes, une
chambre haute et un Roi. On s'occupe a
balancer ces différens pouvoirs; comme ſi
cet équilibre de forces, qu'on a pu croire
neceſſaire pour balancer l'énorme prépon-
dérance de la Royauté, pouvoit être de
quelque uſage dans des Républiques fondées
ſur l'égalité de tous les citoyens; et comme
ſi tout ce qui établit différens corps n'êtoit
pas une ſource de diviſions. En voulant
prévenir des dangers chimériques, on en
fait naitre de réels; on veut n'avoir rien à
craindre du clergé, on le réunit ſous la
barriere d'une proſcription commune. En
l'excluant du droit d'éligibilité, on en fait
un corps, et un corps étranger à l'Etat.
Pourquoi un citoyen, qui a le même interêt que les autres à la defenſe commune
de ſa liberté et de ſes propriétés, eſt-il
exclus d'y contribuer de ſes lumieres et de
ſes vertus, parce qu'il eſt d'une profeſſion
qui exige des lumieres et des vertus? Le
clergé n'eſt dangereux que quand il exiſte
en corps dans l'Etat; que quand il croit
avoir en corps des droits et des interêts,
que quand on a imaginé d'avoir une religion
établie par la loi, comme ſi les hommes

pouvoient

pouvoient avoir quelque droit, ou quelque
interêt à régler la confcience les uns des
autres ; comme fi l'individu pouvoit facri-
fier aux avantages de la focieté civile les
opinions auxquelles il croit fon falut éter-
nel attaché ; comme fi l'on fe fauvoit, ou fe
damnoit, en commun. Là où la vraye tolé-
rance, c'eft-à-dire l'incompétence abfolue
du gouvernement fur la confcience des individus, eft établie, l'ecclefiaftique au milieu
de l'affemblée nationale n'eft qu'un citoyen, lorfqu'il y eft admis ; il redevient
ecclefiaftique lorfqu'on l'en exclut.

Je ne vois pas qu'on fe foit affez occupé
de réduire au plus petit nombre poffible,
les genres d'affaires dont le gouvernement
de chaque Etat fera chargé ; ni à féparer les
objets de légiflation, de ceux d'adminiftration générale et de ceux d'adminiftration
particuliere et locale ; à conftituer des affemblées locales fubfiftantes, qui rem-
pliffant prefque toutes les fonctions de
detail du gouvernement difpenfent les
affemblées générales de s'en occuper, et
ôtent aux membres de celles-ci tout
moyen, et peut-être tout défir d'abufer
d'une autorité qui ne peut s'appliquer qu'à

des

des objets généraux et par là même étrangers aux petites paſſions qui agitent les hommes.

Je ne vois pas qu'on ait fait attention à la grande diſtinction la ſeule fondée ſur la nature entre deux claſſes d'hommes, celle des propriétaires de terres, et celle des non-propriétaires ; à leurs interets et par conſé-quent à leurs droits différens, relativement à la légiſlation, à l'adminiſtration de la juſ-tice et de la police, à la contribution aux dépenſes publiques et à leur emploi.

Nul principe fixe établi ſur l'impôt ; on ſuppoſe que chaque province peut ſe taxer à ſa fantaiſie, établir des taxes perſonnelles, des taxes ſur les conſommations, ſur les importations, c'eſt-à-dire ſe donner un interêt contraire à l'interêt des autres provinces.

On ſuppoſe par tout le droit de régler le commerce ; on autoriſe même les corps exe-cutifs, ou les gouverneurs à prohiber l'ex-portation de certaines denrées dans certaines occurrences ; tant on eſt loin d'avoir ſenti que la loi de la liberté entiere de tout com-merce eſt un corollaire du droit de pro-priété ; tant on eſt encore plongé dans le brouillard des illuſions Européennes.

Dans

Dans l'union générale des provinces entre elles, je ne vois point une coalition, une
fufion de toutes les parties, qui n'en faffe
qu'un corps *un*, et homogene. Ce n'eft
qu'une aggrégation de parties, toujours trop
féparées, et qui confervent toujours une
tendance à fe divifer, par la diverfité de
leurs loix, de leurs mœurs, de leurs opinions ;
par l'inégalité de leurs forces actuelles ; plus
encore par l'inégalité de leurs progrès ulté-
rieurs. Ce n'eft qu'une copie de la Ré-
publique Hollandoife ; et celle-ci même
n'avoit pas à craindre comme la Républ-
ique Américaine les accroiffemens pof-
fibles de quelques unes de fes provinces.
Tout cet édifice eft appuyé jufqu'à pré-
fent fur la bâfe fauffe de la très ancienne et
très vulgaire politique ; fur le prejugé que
les nations, les provinces, peuvent avoir des
interêts, en corps de province et de nation,
autres que celui qu'ont les individus d'être
libres et de défendre leurs propriétés contre
les brigan et les conquerans : interêt prétendu de faire plus de commerce que les
autres, de ne point acheter les marchandifes
de l'étranger, de forcer l'étranger à con-
fommer leurs productions et les ouvrages
de leurs manufactures : interêt prétendu

d'avoir

d'avoir un territoire plus vaſte, d'acquérir
telle ou telle province, telle ou telle iſle, tel
ou tel village : interêt d'inſpirer la crainte
aux autres nations : interêt de l'emporter ſur
elles par la gloire des armes, par celle des
arts et des ſciences.

Quelques-uns de ces préjugés ſont fo-
mentés en Europe, parce que la rivalité
ancienne des nations et l'ambition des
princes oblige tous les Etats à ſe tenir armés
pour ſe défendre contre leurs voiſins armés,
et à regarder la force militaire comme l'objet
principal du gouvernement. L'Amérique a
le bonheur de ne pouvoir avoir d'ici à bien
longtems d'ennemi extérieur à craindre, ſi
elle ne ſe diviſe elle même ; ainſi elle peut
et doit apprécier à leur juſte valeur ces prétendus interêts, ces ſujets de diſcorde qui
ſeuls ſont à redouter pour ſa liberté. Avec
le principe ſacré de la liberté du commerce
regardé comme une ſuite du droit de la
proprieté, tous les prétendus interêts de
commerce diſparoiſſent. Les prétendus interêts de poſſeder plus ou moins de territoires s'évanouiſſent par le principe que le
territoire n'appartient point aux nations,
mais aux individus propriétaires des terres ;

O   que

que la queſtion de ſavoir ſi tel canton, tel village, doit appartenir à telle province, à tel Etat ne doit point être décidée par le prétendu interêt de cette province ou de cet Etat, mais par celui qu'ont les habitans de tel canton ou de tel village de ſe raſſembler pour leurs affaires dans le lieu où il leur eſt le plus commode d'aller ; que cet interêt étant meſuré par le plus ou moins de chemin qu'un homme peut faire loin de ſon domicile pour traiter quelques affaires plus importantes ſans trop nuire à ſes affaires journalieres, devient une meſure naturelle et phyſique de l'étendue des juriſdictions et des Etats, et établit entre tous un équilibre d'étendue et de forces, qui écarte tout danger d'inégalité, et toute prétention à la ſupériorité.

L'interêt d'etre craint eſt nul quand on ne demande rien à perſonne, et quand on eſt dans une poſition où l'on ne peut être attaqué par des forces conſidérables avec quelque eſpérance de ſuccès.

La gloire des armes ne vaut pas le bonheur de vivre en paix. La gloire des arts, des ſciences appartient à quiconque veut s'en ſaiſir ; il y a dans ce genre à moiſſonner pour

tout

tout le monde ; le champ des découvertes
eſt inépuiſable, et tous profitent des découvertes des tous.

J'imagine que les Américains n'en ſont
pas encore à ſentir toutes ces verités,
comme il faut qu'ils les ſentent pour aſſurer
le bonheur de leur poſtérité. Je ne blâme
pas leurs chefs. Il a fallu pourvoir au
beſoin du moment par une union telle
quelle, contre un ennemi préſent et redou-
table ; on n'avoit pas le tems de ſonger à
corriger les vices des conſtitutions et de la
compoſition des différens etats. Mais ils
doivent craindre de les éterniſer, et s'occuper des moyens de réunir les opinions et
les interêts et de les ramener à des principes uniformes dans toutes leurs provinces.

Ils ont à cet égard de grands obſtacles à
vaincre.

En Canada, la conſtitution du clergé Romain, et l'exiſtence d'un corps de nobleſſe.

Dans la Nouvelle Angleterre, l'eſprit encore ſubſiſtant du Puritaniſme rigide, et
toujours, dit on, un peu intolérant.

Dans

Dans la Penfylvanie, un très grand nombre de citoyens établiffant en principe religieux que la profeffion des armes eft illicite, et fe refufant par conféquent aux arrangemens néceffaires pour que le fondement de la force militaire de l'Etat, foit la réunion de la qualité de citoyen avec celle d'homme de guerre et de milicien ; ce qui oblige à faire du métier de la guerre un métier de mercenaires.

Dans les colonies méridionales, une trop grande inégalité de fortunes, et fur tout le grand nombre d'efclaves noirs dont l'efclavage eft incompatible avec une bonne conftitution politique, et qui même en leur rendant la liberté embarrafferont encore en formant deux nations dans le même Etat.

Dans toutes, les préjugés, l'attachement aux formes établies, l'habitude de certaines taxes, la crainte de celles qu'il faudroit y fubftituer, la vanité des colonies qui fe font cru les plus puiffantes, et un malheureux commencement d'orgueil national. Je crois les Américains forcés à s'agrandir, non pas par la guerre, mais par la culture. S'ils

laiffoient

laiſſoient derriere eux les déſerts immenſes
qui s'étendent juſqu'à la mer de l'Oueſt
il s'y etabliroit du mélange de leurs banriis,
et des mauvais ſujets échappés à la ſéverité
des loix, avec les ſauvages : des peuplades
de brigands qui ravageroient l'Amérique,
comme les barbares du nord ont ravagé
l'empire Romain ; de là un autre danger,
la néceſſité de ſe tenir en armes ſur la fron-
tiere et d'être dans un état de guerre con-
tinuelle. Les colonies voiſines de la fron-
tiere ſeroient en conſéquence plus aguerries
que les autres, et cette inégalité dans la
force militaire ſeroit un aiguillon terrible
pour l'ambition. Le remede à cette inégalité ſeroit d'entretenir une force militaire
ſubſiſtante à laquelle toutes les provinces
contribueroient en raiſon de leur population ;
et les Américains qui ont encore toutes les
craintes que doivent avoir les Anglois re-
doutent plus que toute choſe une armée per-
manente. Ils ont tort. Rien n'eſt plus aiſé
que de lier la conſtitution d'une armée perma-
nente avec la milice, de façon que la milice
en devienne meilleure, et que la liberté n'en
ſoit que plus affermie. Mais il éſt mal aiſé
de calmer ſur cela leurs allarmes.

I   Voila

Voila bien des difficultés, et peut-être les interêts fecrets des particuliers puiffans fe joindront-ils aux préjugés de la multitude pour arrêter les efforts des vrais fages et des vrais citoyens.

Il eft impoffible de ne pas faire des vœux pour que ce peuple parvienne à toute la profpérité dont il eft fuceptible. Il eft l'efpérance du genre humain. Il peut en devenir le modéle. Il doit prouver au monde, par le fait, que les hommes peuvent être libres et tranquilles, et peuvent fe paffer des chaines de toute efpece que les tyrans et les charlatans de toute robe ont prétendu leur impôfer fous le pretexte du bien public. Il doit donner l'exemple de la liberté politique, de la liberté religieufe, de la liberté du commerce et de l'induftrie. L'afyle qu'il ouvre à tous les opprimés de toutes les nations doit confoler la terre. La facilité d'en profiter pour fe dérober aux fuites d'un mauvais gouvernement forcera les gouvernemens d'être juftes, et de s'éclairer ; le refte du monde ouvrira peu-à-peu les yeux fur le néant des illufions dont les politiques fe font bercés. Mais il faut pour cela que l'Amérique s'en garantiffe, et qu'elle ne redevienne pas

comme

comme l'ont tant repeté vos écrivains mi-
nifteriels une image de notre Europe, un
amas de puiffances divifées, fe difputant
des territoires ou des profits de commerce,
et cimentant continuellement l'efclavage des
peuples par leur propre fang.

Tous les hommes eclairés, tous les amis
de l'humanité devroient en ce moment réunir leurs lumieres et joindre leurs réfle-
xions à celles des fages Américains pour
concourir au grand ouvrage de leur légiflation. Cela feroit digne de vous, Monfieur ; je voudrois pouvoir échauffer votre
zêle ; et fi dans cette lettre je me fuis livré
plus que je ne l'aurois dû peut-être à l'effufion de mes propres idées, ce défir a été
mon unique motif, et m'excufera à ce
que j'efpere de l'ennui que je vous aurai
caufé. Je voudrois que le fang qui a coulé,
qui coulera encore dans cette querelle
ne fût pas inutile au bonheur du genre
humain.

Nos deux nations vont fe faire récipro-
quement bien du mal, probablement fans
qu'aucune d'elles en retire un profit réel.
L'accroiffement des dettes et des charges,

**

* * * * * * * * * * * * * *, et la ruine
d'un grand nombre de citoyens en feront
peut-être l'unique refultat. L'Angleterre
m'en paroit plus près encore que la France.
Si au lieu de cette guerre vous aviez pu
vous exécuter de bonne grace dès le premier
moment, s'il êtoit donné à la politique de
faire d'avance ce qu'elle fera infailliblement
forcée de faire plus tard, fi l'opinion nationale avoit pu permettre à votre gouvernement de prévenir les evenemens, en
fuppofant qu'il les eut prévus, s'il eût
pu confentir d'abord à l'indépendance de
l'Amérique fans faire la guerre à perfonne,
je crois fermement que votre nation n'auroit rien perdu à ce changement. Elle y
perdra aujourd'hui ce qu'elle a dépenfé, ce
qu'elle dépenfera encore ; elle eprouvera
une grande diminution pour quelque tems
dans fon commerce, de grands boulever-
femens intérieurs fi elle eft forcée à la ban-
queroute ; et quoiqu'il arrive une grande
diminution dans l'influence politique au
dehors, mais ce dernier article eft d'une
bien petite importance pour le bonheur
réel d'un peuple, et je ne fuis point du tout
de l'avis de l'Abbé Rainal dans votre épi-
graphe. Je ne crois point que ceci vous
mene

mene à devenir une nation meprifable, et
vous jette dans l'efclavage.

Vos malheurs feront peut-être au contraire l'effet d'une amputation néceffaire ;
ils font peut-être le feul moyen de vous
fauver de la cangrene du luxe et de la
corruption. Si dans vos agitations vous
pouviez corriger votre conftitution en rendant les elections annuelles, en repartiffant
le droit de repréfentation d'une maniere
plus égale et plus proportionnée aux interets des repréfentés, vous gagneriez
peut-être autant que l'Amérique à cette
révolution ; car votre liberté vous refteroit,
et vos autres pertes fe répareroient bien
vîte avec elle et par elle.

Vous devez juger, Monfieur, par la fran-
chife avec laquelle je m'ouvre à vous fur ces
points délicats, de l'eftime que vous m'avéz
infpirée, et de la fatisfaction que j'eprouve
à penfer quil y a quelque reffemblance entre
nos manieres de voir. Je compte bien que
cette confidence n'eft que pour vous.
Je vous prie même de ne point me répondre
en détail par la pofte, car votre réponfe feroit
infailliblement ouverte dans nos bureaux

P   de

de poſte, et l'on me trouveroit beaucoup trop ami de la liberté pour un miniſtre, même pour un miniſtre diſgracié !

J'ai l'honneur d'etre, Monſieur, avec toute la conſideration poſſible,

Votre très' humble,

et très obeiſſant ſerviteur,

T U R G O T.

It is not eaſy to do juſtice in Engliſh *to many parts of the preceding letter. The following Tranſlation of it will however, I hope, be found to be nearly correct; and I think myſelf greatly obliged to the Gentleman who has been ſo good as to favour me with it.*

To

TRANSLATION.

To Dr. PRICE, *London.*

Paris, 22d March, 1778.

SIR,

MR. FRANKLIN by your defire has put into my hands the laft edition of your *Obfervations on Civil Liberty,* &c. for which I think myfelf doubly indebted to you. In the firft place, for the work itfelf, of which I have long known the value and read with great avidity, notwithftanding the multiplicity of my engagements, when it was firft publifhed: And in the next place, for the politenefs you have fhewn in leaving out the imputation of *want of addrefs,* * which you intermixed

P 2   with

---

* What is here faid refers to the following account of M. *Turgot's* adminiftration in the *fecond* tract on *Civil Liberty and the War with America,* p. 150, &c. " A new reign produced a new minifter of finance in " *France,* whofe name will be refpected by pofterity for " a fet of meafures as new to the *political* world, as any " late difcoveries in the fyftem of nature have been to the " *philofophical* world—Doubtful in their oparation, as " all

with the handfome things you faid of me
in your additional obfervations. I might
have merited this imputation, if you
had in view no other *want of addrefs*
than incapacity to unravel the fprings
of thofe intrigues that were employed
againft me, by fome people who are
much more expert in thefe matters than
I am, or ever fhall be, or indeed ever defire to be : But I imagined you imputed to
me *a want of addrefs* which made my opinions

" all untried meafures muft be, but diftinguifhed by
" their tendency to lay a folid foundation for endlefs
" peace, induftry, and a general enjoyment of the gifts
" of nature, arts and commerce—The edicts iffued dur-
" ing his adminiftration exhibit indeed a *phænomenon* of
" the moft extraordinary kind. An abfolute King ren-
" dering a voluntary account to his fubjects, and inci-
" ting his people to *think*; a right which it has been the
" bufinefs of all abfolute princes and their mininfters to
" extinguifh.—In thefe edicts the King declared in the
" moft diftinct terms againft a bankruptcy, &c. while
" the minifter applied himfelf to increafe every public
" refource by principles more liberal than *France*, or any
" part of *Europe*, ever had in ferious contemplation.—
" It is much to be regretted, that the oppofition he met
" with and the intrigues of a court fhould have deprived
" the world of thofe lights, which muft have refulted from
" the example of fuch an adminiftration." In this paffage
I had, in the firft edition, mentioned improperly Mr.
Turgot's

nions grofsly claſh with the general opinions of my countrymen; and in that refpeſt
I thought you neither did juſtice to *me* nor
to *my country*, where there is a degree of
underſtanding much fuperior to what you
generally fuppofe in England, and where it
is more eafy perhaps, than even with you,
to bring back the public to hearken to
reafon.

I have been led to judge thus by the infatuation of your people in the abfurd projeſt of
fubduing America, till the affair of Bur-

Turgot's want of addrefs among the other caufes of his
difmiffion from power. This occafioned a letter from
him to inform me of the true reafons of his difmiffion,
and begun that correfpondence, of which this letter is a
part, and which continued till his death.—It may not
be improper to add here, that his fucceffor was Mr.
Necker, author of the interefting Treatife on the Adminiftration of the Finances of France juft publiſhed; and
that in the paffage juft quoted, the following notice is taken of this appointment.—" After a ſhort in-
" terval, a nomination, in fome refpeſts ſtill more ex-
" traordinary, took place in the Court of *France*. A
" court, which a few years fince was diftinguiſhed by its
" bigotry and intolerance, has raifed a *proteſtant*, the fub-
" jeſt of a fmall but virtuous republic, to a decifive lead
" in the regulation of its finances. It is to be prefumed
" that fo fingular a preference will produce an equally
" fingular exertion of integrity and talents."

goyne

goyne began to open their eyes ; and by
the fyftem of monopoly and exclufion which
has been recommended by all your writers on
Commerce, (except Mr. Adam Smith and
Dean Tucker) ; a fyftem which has been the
true fource of your feparation from your Colonies. I have alfo been led to this opinion by
all your controverfial writings upon the queftions which have occupied your attention thefe
twenty years, and in which, till your obfervations appeared, I fcarce recollect to have read
one that took up thefe queftions on their proper
ground. I cannot conceive how a nation which
has cultivated every branch of natural knowledge with fuch fuccefs, fhould have made
fo little progrefs in the moft interefting
of all fciences, that of the public good : A
fcience, in which the liberty of the Prefs,
which fhe alone enjoys, ought to have given
her a prodigious advantage over every other
nation in Europe. Was it national pride
which prevented you from profiting by this
advantage ? Or was it, becaufe you were
not altogether in fo bad a condition as other
nations, that you have impofed upon your-
felves in your fpeculations fo far as to be perfuaded that your arrangements were com-
pleat ? Is it party fpirit and a defire of being

I   fupported

supported by popular opinion which has retarded your progress, by inducing your political writers to treat as vain Metaphysics * all thofe fpeculations which aim at eftablifh-ing the rights and true interefts of nations and individuals upon fixed principles. How comes it that you are almoft the firft of the writers of your country, who has given a juft idea of liberty, and fhewn the falfity of the notion fo frequently repeated by almoft all Republican Writers, " that liberty con-" fifts in being fubject only to the laws," as if a man could be free while oppreffed by an unjuft law. This would not be true, even if we could fuppofe that all the laws were the work of an affembly of the whole nation; for certainly every individual has his rights, of which the nation cannot de-prive him, except by violence and an un-lawful ufe of the general power. Though you have attended to this truth and have ex-plained yourfelf upon this head, perhaps it would have merited a more minute expla-nation, confidering how little attention is paid to it even by the moft zealous friends of liberty.

It is likewife extraordinary that it was not thought a trivial matter in England to affert

---

* See Mr. Burke's Letter to the Sheriffs of Briftol.

" that

" that one nation never can have a right to
" govern another nation"—" that a govern-
" ment where fuch a principle is admitted
" can have no foundation but that of force,
" which is equally the foundation of robbery
" and tyranny"—" and that the tyranny of
" a people is the moft cruel and intolerable,
" becaufe it leaves the feweft refources to the
" oppreffed."—A defpot is reftrained by a
fenfe of his own intereft. He is checked by
remorfe or by the public opinion. But the
multitude never calculate. The multitude are
never checked by remorfe, and will even af-
cribe to themfelves the higheft honour when
they deferve only difgrace.

What a dreadful commentary on your
book are the events which have lately be-
fallen the Englifh nation ?——For fome
months they have been running head-
long to ruin.—The fate of America is already decided—Behold her independent beyond recovery.—But will She be free and
happy ?—Can this new people, fo advan-
tageoufly placed for giving an example to the
world of a conftitution under which man
may enjoy his rights, freely exercife all
his faculties, and be governed only by nature, reafon and juftice—Can they form fuch
a Conftitution ?—Can they eftablifh it upon
a never-

a neverfailing foundation, and guard againft every fource of divifion and corruption which may gradually undermine and deftroy it ?

I confefs that I am not fatisfied with the Conftitutions which have hitherto been formed by the different States of America. It is with reafon that you reproach the State of Penfylvania with exacting a religious teft from thofe who become members of the body of Reprefentatives. There are much worfe tefts in the other States; and there is one (I believe the Jerfeys) which requires (†) a declaration of faith in the *Divinity* of Jefus Chrift.—I obferve that by moft of them the cuftoms of England are imitated, without any particular motive. Inftead of collecting all authority into one center, that of the nation, they have eftablifhed different bodies; a body of reprefentatives, a council, and a Governour, becaufe there is in England a Houfe of Commons, a Houfe of Lords, and a King.—They endeavour to balance thefe different powers,

(†) It is the Conftitution of *Delware* that impofes the teft here meant. That of the *Jerfeys*, with a noble liberality, orders that there fhall never in that Province be any eftablifhment of any one religious fect in preference to another, and that all Proteftants of all perfuafions fhall enjoy equal rights and privileges.

Q

as

as if this equilibrium, which in *England* may be a neceſſary check to the enormous influence of royalty, could be of any uſe in Republics founded upon the equality of all the Citizens; and as if eſtabliſhing different orders of men, was not a ſource of diviſions and diſputes. In attempting to prevent imaginary dangers they create real ones; and in their deſire to have nothing to fear from the clergy, they unite them more cloſely by one common proſcription. By excluding them from the right of being elected into public offices they become a body diſtinct from the State. Wherefore ſhould a Citizen, who has the ſame intereſt with others in the common defence of liberty and property, be excluded from contributing to it his virtue and knowledge? Is it becauſe he is of a profeſſion which *requires* knowledge and virtue? The clergy are only dangerous when they exiſt as a diſtinct body in the State; and think themſelves poſſeſſed of ſeparate rights and intereſts and a religion eſtabliſhed by law, as if ſome men had a right to regulate the conſciences of other men, or could have an intereſt in doing this; as if an individual could ſacrifice to civil ſociety opinions on which he thinks his

eternal

eternal falvation depends ; as if, in fhort, mankind were to be faved or *damned* in *communities*—Where *true* toleration, (that is, where the abfolute incompetency of civil government in matters of confcience, is eftablifhed); there the *clergyman*, when admitted into the national affembly, becomes a *fimple citizen*; but when excluded, he becomes an *ecclefiaftic*.

I do not think they are fufficiently careful to reduce the kind of bufinefs with which the government of each State is charged, within the narroweft limits poffible; nor to feparate the objects of legiflation from thofe of the general adminiftration, or from thofe of a local and particular adminiftration; nor to inftitute local permanent affemblies, which by difcharging almoft all the functions in the detail of government, make it unneceffary for the general affemblies to attend to thefe things, and thereby deprive the members of the general affemblies of every means, and perhaps every defire, of abufing a power which can only be applied to general objects, and which, confequently, muft be free from the influence of the little paffions by which men ufually are agitated.

I do

I do not find that they attend to the great diftinction (the only one which is founded in nature between two claffes of men), between landholders, and thofe who are not landholders; to their interefts, and of courfe to their different rights refpecting legiflation, the adminiftration of juftice and police, their contributions to the public expence, and employment.

No fixed principle of taxation is eftablifhed. They fuppofe that each State may tax itfelf according to its own fancy, by eftablifhing either *perfonal* taxes, or taxes on *confumption* and *importation* ; that is, that each State may affume to itfelf an intereft contrary to the intereft of the other States.

They alfo every where fuppofe that they have a right to regulate commerce. They even delegate authority to executive bodies, and to Governors, to prohibit the exportation of certain commodities on certain occafions. So far are they from being fenfible that the right to an entire liberty in commerce is the confequence of the right of property. So much are they ftill involved in the mift of European illufions.

In the general union of the States I do not obferve a coalition, a fufion of all the

5

parts to form one homogeneous body. It is only a jumble of communities too difcordant, and which retain a conftant tendency to feparation, owing to the diverfity in their laws, cuftoms and opinions ; to the inequality in their *prefent* ftrength ; but ftill more, to the inequality in their advances to *greater* ftrength. It is only a copy of the Dutch republic, with this difference, that the *Dutch* republic had nothing to fear, as the *American* republic has, from the future poffible increafe of any one of the Provinces.—All this edifice has been hitherto fupported upon the erroneous foundation of the moft ancient and vulgar policy ; upon the prejudice that Nations and States, as fuch, may have an intereft diftinct from the intereft which individuals have to be free, and to defend their property againft the attacks of robbers and conquerors : An intereft, in carrying on a more extenfive commerce than other States, in not purchafing foreign merchandize, and compelling foreigners to confume their produce and manufactures : An intereft in poffeffing more extenfive territories, and acquiring fuch and fuch a province, ifland or village: An intereft in infpiring other nations with awe, and gaining a

fuperiority

superiority over them in the glory of arts, sciences, and arms.

Some of these prejudices are fomented in *Europe*, from the ancient rivalship of nations and the ambition of Princes, which compel every State to keep up an armed force to defend itself against the attack of neighbours in arms, and to look upon a military force as the principal object of government. *America* is likely in no long time to enjoy the happiness of having no external enemy to dread, provided she is not divided within herself. She ought, therefore, to estimate properly those pretended *interests* and causes of discord which alone are likely to be formidable to her liberty. On that sacred principle, " liberty of commerce " considered as a natural right flowing from " the possession of property," all the pretended interests of commerce must vanish.— The supposed interest in possessing more or less territory disappear on this principle, " that a territory does not belong to na- " tions, but to the individuals who are pro- " prietors of the lands." The question, whether such a canton or such a village belongs to such a Province or such a State, ought not to be determined by the interest in it pretended by that Province or that

State ;

State; but by the intereft the inhabitants of the canton or village have in affembling for tranfacting their affairs in the place moft convenient for them. This intereft, meafured by the greater or lefs diftance that a man can go from his home to attend to important affairs without injuring his private concerns, forms a natural boundary to the jurifdiction of States, and eftablifhes an equipoife * of extent and ftrength between them, which muft remove every danger of inequality, and every pretence to fuperiority.

There can be no intereft in being feared when nothing can be demanded, and when men are in a fituation not to be attacked by a confiderable force with any hope of fuccefs.

The glory of *arms* is nothing to thofe who enjoy the happinefs of living in peace.

The glory of arts and fciences belongs to every man who can acquire it. There is

---

* This feems to be a particular of much confequence. The great inequality now exifting, and which is likely to increafe, between the different States, is a very unfavourable circumftance; and the embaraffment and danger to which it expofes the union ought to be guarded againft as far as poffible in laying out future States.

here

here ample fcope. The field of difcovery is boundlefs; and all profit by the difcoveries of all.

I imagine that the Americans are not as fenfible of thefe truths, as they ought to be, in order to fecure the happinefs of their pofterity. I do not blame their leaders. It was neceffary to provide for the neceffities of the moment, by fuch an union as they could form againft a prefent and moft formidable enemy. They have not leifure to confider how the errors of the different conftitutions and States may be corrected; but they ought to be afraid of perpetuating thefe errors, and to endeavour by all means to reconcile the opinions and interefts of the different provinces, and to unite them by bringing them to one uniform fet of principles.

To accomplifh this they have great obftacles to furmount.

In Canada, an order of Roman Catholic Clergy, and a body of Nobles.

In New England, a rigid puritanical fpirit which has been always fomewhat intolerant *.

* This has been *once* true of the inhabitants of *New-England*, but it is not fo *now*. See p. 47.

In Penfylvania, a very great number of inhabitants laying it down as a religious principle, that the profeffion of arms is unlaw-
ful, and refufing to join in the arrangements
neceffary to eftablifh the military force of
the State, by uniting the character of the
Citizen with that of the Soldier and Mili-
tiaman, in confequence of which the bufinefs of war is made to be the bufinefs of
mercenaries.

In the Southern Colonies, an inequality
of fortune too great; and what is worfe,
a great number of Blacks, whofe flavery
is incompatible with a good political conftitution; and who, if emancipated, would
occafion great embarraffement by forming
two diftinct people in one State.

In all of them, various prejudices, an attachment to eftablifhed forms, a habit of
paying certain taxes, and a dread of thofe
which muft be fubftituted for them; a
vanity in thofe colonies which think themfelves moft powerful; and a wretched beginning of national pride. I imagine that
the Americans muft aggrandize themfelves
not by war, but by agriculture. If they
neglect the immenfe defarts which are at
their backs, and which extend all the way

R   to

to the weſtern ſea, their exiles and fugi-
tives from the ſeverity of the laws, will
unite with the Savages, and ſettle that part
of the country; the conſequence of which
will be that bodies of Banditti will
ravage America, as the Barbarians of the
North ravaged the Roman Empire, and
ſubject the States to the neceſſity of keeping the frontiers always guarded, and remaining in a State of continual war. The
Colonies next to the frontier will of courſe
be better diſciplined than the reſt; and
this inequality of military force will prove
a dreadful incentive to ambition. The
remedy for this inequality would be to
keep up a ſtanding army, to which every
State ſhould contribute in proportion to
its population; but the Americans, who
have the fears that the Engliſh *ought* to
have, dread nothing ſo much as a ſtanding army. In this they are wrong. There
is nothing more eaſy than to combine a
ſtanding army with a militia, ſo as to improve the militia, and gain additional ſecurity for liberty. But it is no eaſy matter
to calm their apprehenſions on that head.

Here are a number of difficulties; and
perhaps the private intereſts of powerful
individuals

individuals will unite with the prejudices of the multitude, to check the efforts of true Philofophers and good Citizens.

It is impoffible not to wifh ardently that this people may attain to all the profperity of which they are capable. They are the *hope* of the world. They may become a *model* to it. They *may* prove by fact that men can be free and yet tranquil ; and that it is in their power to refcue themfelves from the chains in which tyrants and knaves of all defcriptions have prefumed to bind them under the pretence of the public good. They may exhibit an example of *political* liberty, of *religious* liberty, of *commerical* liberty, and of induftry. The *Afylum* they open to the oppreffed of all nations fhould confole the earth. The eafe with which the injured may efcape from oppreffive governments, will compel Princes to become juft and cautious ; and the reft of the world will gradually open their eyes upon the empty illufions with which they have been hitherto cheated by politicians. But for this purpofe *America* muft preferve *herfelf* from thefe illufions ; and take care to avoid being what your minifterial writers are fre-

R 2   quently

quently faying She *will* be—an image of our
Europe—a mafs of divided powers contending for territory and commerce, and continually cementing the flavery of the people
with their own blood.

All enlightened men—All the friends of
humanity ought at this time to unite their
lights to thofe of the *American* fages, and
to affift them in the great work of legiflation. This, fir, would be a work worthy
of you. I wifh it was in my power to ani-
mate your zeal in this inftance. If I have in
this letter indulged too free an effufion
of my fentiments, this has been my only
motive; and it will, I hope, induce you to
pardon me for tiring you. I wifh indeed
that the blood which has been fpilt, and
which will contiune for fome time to be
fpilt in this conteft, may not be without its
ufe to the human race.

Our two nations are about doing much
harm to each other, and probably without
the profpect to either of any real advantage.
An increafe of debts and public burthens,
(perhaps a national bankruptcy), and the
ruin of a great number of individuals, will
prove the refult. England feems to me to
be more likely to fuffer by thefe evils,
and much nearer to them, than France.
—If

—If inftead of going to war, you had at the commencement of your difputes endeavoured to retreat with a good grace ; if your Statef-men had then confented to make thofe conceffions, which they will infallibly be obliged to make at laft ; if the national opinion would have permitted your govern-ment to anticipate events which might have been forefeen ; if, in fhort, you had immediately yielded to the independence of America without entering into any hoftili-ties ; I am firmly perfuaded your nation would have loft nothing.—But you will *now* lofe what you have already expended, and what you are ftill to expend ; you will ex-perience a great diminution of your com-merce for fome time, and great interior commotions, if driven to a bankruptcy; and, at any rate, a great diminution of weight in foreign politics. But this laft circum-ftance I think of little confequence to the real happinefs of a people ; for I cannot agree with the *Abbe Raynal* in your motto*.

I do

* This refers to the following words (taken from Mr. Juftamond's tranflation of the *Abbe Raynal's* Hiftory of the European Settlements) in the Title-page to the Second Tract on Civil Liberty—" Should the morals " of the Englifh be perverted by luxury—fhould they " lofe

I do not believe all this will make you a contemptible nation or throw you into flavery.—On the contrary; your misfortunes may have the effect of a neceſſary amputation. They are perhaps the only means of faving you from the gangrene of luxury and corruption. And if they fhould terminate in the amendment of your conſtitution, by reſtoring annual elections, and diſtributing the right of fuffrages for reprefentation fo as to render it more equal and better proportioned to the intereſts of the reprefented, you will perhaps gain as much as America by this revolution; for you will preferve your liberty, and with your liberty, and by means of it, all your other loſſes will be fpeedily repaired.

By the freedom with which I have opened myſelf to you, fir, upon thefe delicate points, you will judge of the eſteem with which you have infpired me; and the fatisfaction I feel in thinking there is fome re-

____

" lofe their colonies by reſtraining them, &c. they will
" be enflaved. They will become infignificant and
" contemptible; and Europe will not be able to fhew
" the world *one* nation in which fhe can pride herfelf."

femblance

femblance between our fentiments and views.
I depend on your * confining this confidence
to yourfelf. I even beg that you will not
be particular in anfwering me by the Poft,
for your letter will certainly be opened at
our Poft-Offices, and I fhall be found much
too great a friend to liberty for a minifter,
even though a difcarded minifter.

I have the honour to be with all poffible refpect,

Sir,

Your moft humble,

and moft obedient Servant,

T U R G O T.

---

* In compliance with Mr. *Turgot*'s defire, this letter was kept private during his life. Since his death I
have thought the publication of it a duty which I owe
to his memory, as well as to the United States and
the world. I can add, with much fatisfaction, that my
venerable friend and the excellent Philofopher and
Satefman whofe name introduces this letter; and
alfo, that fome intimate friends of Mr. *Turgot*'s, who
have been confulted on this fubject, concur with me in
this fentiment.

Note omitted in Page 52.

The imperfection of *real* knowledge may often produce
unreafonable incredulity.——Had the beft Philofophers
been told a few years ago, " that there exifted fifhes which
" had the command of *lightening*, and which ufed it to
" kill their prey," they would have fcouted the information as abfurd and ridiculous.

E R R A T A.

P. 148. *For* tranſacting in buſineſs, *read* tranſacting buſineſs.

P. 153. In lines 5th and 8th, for the numbers 131,501, 139,560, and 143,890, *read* 13,150, 13,956, and 14,389.

A P P E N D I X,

CONTAINING

A Translation from the French of

THE TESTAMENT

O F

M. FORTUNÉ RICARD,

Teacher of Arithmetic at D——.

Read and publifhed at the Court of Bailiwick of that
Town, the 19th of August, 1784.

PRINTED IN M.DCC.LXXXV.

ADVERTISEMENT.

*T*H E *following* Teftament *was lately
publifhed in* France, *and conveyed to
me by* Dr. FRANKLIN. *It exemplifies, with
an inftructive pleafantry and great force, the
account in page* 10, &c. *of the powers of Compound Intereft or a* Sinking Fund, *and the
ufes to which they may be applied for the benefit
of nations and of pofterity. For this reafon I
here offer to the public the following tranflation of it, not doubting but I fhall be excufed if
the turn of humour in it renders it a compo-
fition of a nature not perfectly fuitable to the
other parts of this pamphlet.*

T H E

TESTAMENT, &c.

---

*I*N *the name of God*, I *Fortuné Ricard*, Teacher
of Arithmetic at D——, invoking the Holy
Virgin and Saint *Fortune* my patron, do make
this my laſt Will as follows——

[" The Executors, who have cauſed this Will
" to be printed in order to fulfil the intentions
" of the late *M. Fortuné Ricard*, do not think it
" neceſſary to publiſh thoſe particular bequeſts
" which concern only his own family.—After
" having diſpoſed of his patrimony among them
" with wiſdom, he proceeds in the following man-
" ner."]

It remains now for me to declare my intentions with regard to the promiſe of 500
livres *, ſubſcribed on my behalf by M. P.
banker

* 22 *l.* 4 *s.* 6 *d.*

banker of this town. This fum proceeded originally from a prefent which was made me by *Prof-
per Ricard*, my much honoured grandfather, when
I entered the eighth year of my age. At that
age he had taught me the principles of writing
and calculation. After having fhewn me that a
capital, with its accumulating intereft at five *per
cent.* would amount at the end of 100 years to
more than 131 times the original fum*, and feeing
that I liftened to this lecture with the greateft
attention, he took 24 livres † out of his pocket, and
addreffed me with an enthufiafm which is ftill prefent to my mind—" My child, faid he, remember
" while thou liveft, that with œconomy and cal-
" culation nothing is impoffible for man. Here
" are 24 livres which I give thee. Take them to
" a merchant in our neighbourhood, who will
" place them in trade out of regard to me.
" Every year thou fhalt add the intereft to the
" principal. At thy death thou fhalt employ the
" produce in good works for the repofe of thy
" foul and my own."—I have executed this order
with fidelity, and in the courfe of my life I have
planned many projects for employing this money.
Having reached the 71ft year of my age, it a-
mounts to 500 livres ; but as I muft fome time
or other fet bounds to myfelf, I now defire that
it may be divided into five portions of 100 livres ‡
each ; to which the interefts fhall be annually ad-
ded, and the accumulated fums fhall be fucceffive-
ly applied to the following ufes.

1. In a *hundred* years the firft fum of 100 livres
will amount to more than 13,100 livres §, (5822*l.*).

From

---

* See table 1ft annexed to this Will.
† Nearly a guinea.
‡ Four pounds nine fhillings.
§ See table 1ft and 2d.

From this fum a prize of 4000 livres fhall be given for the beft theological differtation, to prove the lawfulnefs of putting out money to inte-reft. Three medals, of 600 livres each, fhall alfo be given for the three differtations which fhall be adjudged the next in merit to the prize-differta-tion. The remainder of the 13,100 livres fhall be expended in printing the prize differtation and extracts from the others. Copies of thefe fhall be fent, *gratis*, to all the bifhops, clergy, and confeffors of the kingdom. I had intended to have fent them alfo into foreign countries; but I ob-ferve that all the univerfities of the chriftian world, excepting thofe of France, have folemnly recog-nized the lawfulnefs of putting money to intereft*; and that it continues neceffary only in this king-dom to explain a queftion in morals fo interefting to the welfare of the State.

2. After *two hundred* years a *fecond* fum of 100 livres, amounting, with its accumulated intereft, to more than 1,700,000 livres †, (756,500*l.*) fhall be employed in eftablifhing a perpetual fund for fourfcore prizes of 1000 livres each, to be diftri-buted annually by the different academies of the kingdom, as follows:—Fifteen prizes for the moft diftinguifhed virtuous actions—fifteen for works of fcience and literature—ten for folutions of queftions in arithmetic and calculation—ten for fuch new proceffes in agriculture as fhall produce the beft crops—ten for mafter-pieces in the fine arts—
and

* See the approbations of the Univerfities of Alcala, Sa-lamanca, Ingolftadt, Fribourg in Brifgaw, Mayence, Co-logne and Treves, printed at the end of a *Treatife upon Ufury and Intereft. Lyon. Bruyfel-Ponthus,* 1776, in 12mo. The firft five of thefe approbations have been depofited in the archives of the confulfhip of the town of Lyons.
† See table 3d and 4th,

and ten to encourage races and other exercifes proper to difplay the force and agility of the body, and to reftore amongft us a tafte for the gymnafium which was in fuch great efteem a-mong the Greeks, and which formerly made fo many heroes.

After *three hundred* years, from another fum of 100 livres, increafed in that time to more than two hundred and twenty - fix millions, (10,057,000 *l.*) there fhall be appropriated 196 millions towards eftablifhing, in the moft con-fiderable places in France, 500 patriotic banks for lending money without intereft; the largeft of which fhall have a fund of ten millions of li-vres, and the fmalleft a fund of 100,000 livres. Thefe banks fhall be managed by a committee of the moft upright citizens in each place, and the money fhall be employed in loans to fuccour the unfortunate, or advanced towards promoting agriculture, trade, and induftry. The remaining thirty millions fhall be expended in founding twelve *mufeums* in the cities of Paris, Lyons, Rouen, Bourdeaux, Rennes, Lifle, Nancy, Tours, Dijon, Thouloufe, Aix, and Grenoble. Each of thefe *mufeums* fhall be placed at the moft agreeable end of the city. Five hundred thoufand livres fhall be expended upon each building, and in the purchafe of grounds which fhall belong to them, and be laid out into botanical and fruit gar-dens, and alfo into kitchen gardens and extenfive walks. To each mufeum fhall be annexed an income of 100,000 livres; and there fhall be lodged and boarded in it forty literary men and artifts of fuperior merit, who, at the time of meals fhall be divided into four tables, that their repafts may be chearful without being too

I   noify.

noify. Each mufeum fhall be provided with fix Secretaries, a defigner and engraver, and four carriages. There fhall be alfo a hall for concerts, a theatre, a chymical laboratory, a cabinet of natural hiftory, a hall for experimental philofophy, and a grand gallery for a common library. A *hundred thoufand* livres fhall be expended on a feparate library for each of thefe eftablifhments. The fame fum fhall be employed in providing them with feparate cabinets of natural hiftory and with philofophical inftruments. And 10,000 livres fhall be referved annually for keeping up and increafing thefe cabinets and philofophical inftruments.*

The libraries fhall always be open to the public. Twenty members of the mufeum fhall be engaged in giving public and gratuitous courfes of lectures upon the foreign languages, and upon all the arts and fciences. The other twenty fhall be engaged in fuch other employments as may be moft ufeful. No one fhall be admitted a member till he has previoufly given proof, not of his rank, defcent, or nobility, but of his morals, and of his never having difhonoured his pen by writing againft † religion and government, or by fatirifing any member of the community. On being admitted he fhall make oath, " That he will " prefer virtue, truth, and his country to every " thing; and the general good of literature to " his own fame." The works of the members of the mufeum fhall be printed at the expence of the

T efta-

---

* See table 5th.

† No good men will ever write againft religion and government. On the contrary; they will do all they can to render them greater bleffings, by fpreading juft notions of them, and clearing them from thofe abufes and corruptions by which ufurpers and hypocrites have made them the means of enflaving and debafing mankind.

eftablifhment, and when thofe expences are reim-
burfed, the profits fhall belong to the authors.

4. After *four hundred* years the fourth fum of 100
livres, amounting, with intereft, to near 30,000 millions, (1,330,000,000*l.*) fhall be employed in building 100 towns, each containing 150,000 fouls *, in
the moft agreeable fituations which can be found
in France. The means of peopling thefe towns,
of governing and making them flourifh, are ex-
plained in a memorial annexed to this will †. In
a fhort time there will refult from hence an addition of 15 millions of inhabitants to the kingdom, and its confumption will be doubled, for
which fervice I hope the œconomifts will think
themfelves obliged to me.

I am fenfible that all the fpecie in Europe is
not equal to thefe 30,000 millions, and that it
will be impoffible to make provifion in money for
fuch immenfe fums. For this reafon I leave it to
the difcretion of my executors to exchange cafh at
convenient feafons for landed and other real poffeffions. The revenue arifing from thofe poffeffions
fhall either be laid out in cafh, or realized by
further purchafes, fo that my bequefts may be
fulfilled in their due time without any difficulty.

I am convinced, by the moft accurate calculations, that my arrangements inftead of clogging
will give activity to the circulation of fpecie.
Laying out the money I have ordered in the purchafe

* See table 6th.
† The Executors have not yet determined whether they
fhall publifh this Memorial, which is very copious, and contains fome ideas that may claim originality. The more im-
mediate concerns of their executorfhip have not yet afforded
them time for examining the whole of it. Befides, there can
be no neceffity of hurrying the publication, inafmuch as
the towns of which it treats are not to be built till the end
of four centuries.

chafe of eftates, will foon increafe their value; and
when thefe accumulating riches fhall have fo produced their effect as that there can no longer be
found in France a landholder who will fell his
eftate, purchafes muft be fought for among the
neighbouring nations.

5. Finally, with regard to the laft fum of 100
livres, amounting nearly, by the accumulation
of *five hundred* years, to four millions of millions of
livres,* it fhall be difpofed of as follows.

Six thoufand millions fhall be appropriated towards paying the national debt of France, upon
condition that the Kings, our good lords and
mafters, fhall be entreated to order the comptrollers general of the finances to undergo in future
an examination in arithmetic † before they enter
upon their office.

Twelve thoufand millions fhall likewife be employed in paying the public debts of England.—
It may be feen that I reckon that both thofe national debts will be *doubled* in this period; not
that I have any doubts of the talents of certain
minifters to increafe them much more, but
their operations in this way are oppofed by an infinity of circumftances which lead me to pre-
fume that thofe debts cannot be more than doubled. Befides, if they amount to a few thoufands
of millions more, I declare that it is my intention
that they fhould be entirely paid off, and that a
project fo laudable fhould not remain unexecuted

T 2 for

---

* 176 thoufands of millions fterling.—See tables 2d and
7th.

† There have been, it is faid, even in ENGLAND Lords
of the Admiralty who could not *count*, and Chancellors of
the *Exchequer* who could not *read* figures.

for a trifle more or lefs. I beg that the Englifh would not refufe this flight mark of the remembrance of a man, who was indeed born a Frenchman, but who fincerely efteemed their nation, and always was a particular admirer of that magnificent work which Newton, their countryman, has entitled *Univerfal Arithmetic.* I earneftly *defire* that, as an acknowledgment for this legacy, the Englifh nation will confent to call the French *their neighbours** and not *their natural enemies*; that they be affured that *nature* never made man an enemy to man; and that national hatreds, commercial prohibitions, and, above all, *wars* conftantly produce a monftrous error in calculations. But I dare not, in this inftance, *require* any thing. We muft hope for all we defire from time; and when we have the happinefs of rendering a fervice, we muft not deftroy its value by annexing conditions to it which may encumber thofe whom we wifh to ferve.

Thirty thoufand millions fhall be formed into a fund for producing an annual revenue of 15 hundred millions to be divided in times of peace among all the powers of Europe. In time of war the fhare of the aggreffor or aggreffors fhall be given to thofe who have been attacked unjuftly, in order to engage fovereigns, if poffible, to reflect a little before they commence unjuft hoftilities. This revenue fhall be diftributed among the different nations in proportion to their population. Every ten years an exact numeration

* The parable of the good Samaritan directs every man to look upon every man as his *neighbour*, without regarding his country or religion. M. *Ricard* appears to have attended to this divine inftruction. But *Englifhmen* probably forget it, when, in their public devotions, they pray that God would *abate the pride* and *affuage the malice* of their enemies,

tion fhall be taken with a view to this diftribution, which fhall be made by a diet compofed of deputies from all the different nations; but I direct that a larger proportion fhall be diftributed to thofe fovereigns who fhall apply for it and appear to defire it with no other view than to encourage population among their fubjects.

I leave to the wifdom of my executors the care of extending the benefits of this bequeft to the other parts of the world; and if, by this means, they fhould hope to fucceed in extinguifhing throughout the world the abfurd and barbarous rage of war, I willingly confent that they appropriate for this purpofe the further fum of one hundred thoufand millions. I wifh that fix thoufand millions may be offered to his Majefty, the King of France; namely, a *thoufand* millions to fuperfede the neceffity of lotteries, a fort of tax impofed upon wicked men which infallibly renders them a great deal more wicked; a *thoufand* millions to buy in all ufelefs offices which are attended with the fad inconvenience of perfuading many perfons that it is a fufficient difcharge of their duty to their country to occupy an office without functions, and that an honour may be derived from bearing a fenfelefs title; a *thoufand* millions to buy in offices which, on the contrary, are too important to be left expofed to the danger of venality; a *thoufand* millions to purchafe a domain for his Majefty worthy of his crown, and fufficient for the expences of his court, fo that the nation may clearly perceive that the taxes impofed upon them are applicable only to the expenditures of the ftate. The remaining two thoufand millions fhall form a fund, whofe annual produce fhall be employed by his Majefty in penfions and gratuities. By thefe means, if fometimes thofe favours

fhould

L

fhould be conferred upon intriguing and unde-
ferving perfons, the nation will have no caufe
to complain of the improper ufe of money drawn
from taxes and the labours of the hufband-
man.

I appoint a *thoufand millions* towards adding a
thoufand *livres* to the fettled income of all the
clergy in the kingdom, and 600 livres to that
of their vicars, upon condition that they no
longer demand fees for faying maffes. I had
alfo fome thoughts of propofing to them the
fuppreffion of fees for baptifms, marriages, and
burials; but I have confidered thofe functions to be of a *civil* as well as *religious* nature;
and that on this account the clergy may, without impropriety, be allowed to receive a pay
which is, in fact, more moderate than would
be required by any other public officers in
their places. Befides, this pay, perhaps, renders the fervice more exact, more fpeedy on
their part, and lefs irkfome to the delicacy of
fome of thofe who receive it.

I appoint two thoufand millions towards
forming an income of *ten* livres a month to
all the children which fhall be born in the
kingdom till they are three years of age; and
I defire this legacy to be increafed to *thirty*
livres a month to thofe children which fhall be
nurfed by their own mothers. I do not except
even the children of the rich; on the contrary, I
invite rich parents to accept this donation without
reluctance, as an honorary prize awarded to pa-
ternity and the cares of maternal love. They may,
if they pleafe, apply it to acts of charity and benevolence.

I appoint four thoufand millions towards
purchafing the wafte lands of the kingdom.
Thefe

Thefe fhall be divided into 500 thoufand little farms or tenements of four or five acres each. on which fhall be erected as many commodious cottages. Thefe 500 thoufand farms fhall be given as freeholds to an equal number of married *peafants*, chofen in each parifh by a veftry compofed of ten of the moft aged inhabitants. The poffeffors of thefe *freeholds* fhall be obliged to make them their only refidence, to cultivate them with their own hands and thofe of their families, and to report every year the improvements of them which they have made. Thefe *freeholds* fhall be hereditary, but only upon condition that they fhall neither be divided, nor any two of them engroffed by one perfon. When a freeholder dies without leaving behind him either wife, children, brothers, fifters, nephews, or nieces, who have lived and laboured with him for three years prior to his deceafe, the freehold fhall be declared vacant, and given anew by the veftry of the parifh to that peafant who fhall appear to deferve it beft.

I defire that two thoufand millions be laid out in purchafing all the manors of which there fhall be fellers, and that the vaffals thereon be for ever afterwards exempted from all fervitude and fealty.

Six thoufand millions fhall be employed in founding houfes of education in all the country parifhes, agreeable to the plan of the author of a work entitled, *Patriotic Views refpecting the Education of the ·People.* If in executing this plan of a man of genius and an excellent citizen it fhould appear to want fome little amendments and alterations, I direct that they fhall be adopted.

I appoint 20,000 millions towards erecting in the kingdom 40,000 houfes of labour, or public work-

work-houfes; to each of which fhall be appropriated from 10,000 to 50,000 livres annual income. Every man and woman fhall have a right
to offer themfelves at any time to be maintained
and employed in them. I chufe to fay nothing
of any other particulars in the government and
management of thefe houfes; hoping that the ideas
which begin to be formed concerning eftablifhments of this kind will be perfected before the period fixed for thefe fhall arrive; and that it will
at length be univerfally acknowledged, that
though it is dangerous and foolifh to give alms
in money to a ftrong beggar, yet that fociety has
no right to deprive him of his liberty and inflict
punifhments upon him, while it does not hold
out to him any other means of fubfiftence, or at
leaft point out to him a method of difcovering
what means he is capable of ufing.

I intreat the managers of thefe public work-
houfes to give the greateft encouragement to fuch
trades as can be performed by women. This fex,
fo dear to all fenfible minds, has been neglected
or oppreffed by all our inftitutions.—Seductions
of all kinds feem to confpire againft their virtue
—Neceffity precipitates them involuntarily into an
abyfs of infamy and mifery.—The low price
which is fet upon the labour of women is out of
all proportion to the inferiority of their bodily
ftrength. Let the public workhoufes fet the example of paying them better.

There are in *France* many houfes of correc-
tion where the mifconduct of women is fe-
verely punifhed, but where in reality it is only
fufpended, mere confinement having no tendency
to eradicate vice. Why fhould there not be *one*
eftablifhment where a young woman, conquered
by temptation and on the brink of defpair, might
present

prefent herfelf, and fay—" Vice offers me gold:
" I only afk for labour and bread, In compaffion.
" to my remorfe affift and ftrengthen me. Open
" an afylum for me where I may weep without
" being feen, expiate thofe faults which purfue
" and overwhelm me, and recover a fhadow of
" peace."—Such an inftitution exifts no where—
I appoint, therefore, a thoufand millions towards
eftablifhing one.

The fnares which are laid by vice for women
without fortunes, would make fewer victims if
more affiftance was given them. We have an
infinity of eftablifhments for perfons in the higher ranks of life which do honour to the generofity
of our forefathers. Why have we none for this
purpofe?—I defire, therefore, that two thoufand
millions be employed in eftablifhing in the kingdom *a hundred* hofpitals, which fhall be called
Hospitals of Angels. There fhall be admitted
into each a hundred females of the age of feven
or eight years, and of the moft engaging forms.
They fhall receive the moft perfect education in
regard to morals, ufeful knowledge, and agreeable
accomplifhments. At the age of eighteen they
may quit the hofpital in order to be married; at
which period they fhall each be paid a portion of
40,000 livres, I mention this moderate fum becaufe it is my wifh that they be neither reproached
for want of fortune, nor efpoufed from intereft.
An annual income of 2000 livres fhall be given
alfo to their parents. * * * * Except once in the year
at a folemn and fplendid proceffion, they fhall rare-
ly appear in public, but fhall be conftantly employed in their afylum in learning all that can render them one day excellent wives and mothers.

In order to fit them, in particular, for *domeftic
œconomy*, I defire that after they have been taught
the moft accurate ideas of expences of all kinds,

queftions

queſtions be propoſed to them from time to time
to which they ſhall be obliged to give anſwers by
word of mouth, and alſo in writing ; as for example—" If you had ſuch or ſuch an income, un-
" der ſuch or ſuch circumſtances, how much
" would you appropriate to your table, your
" houſe-rent, your maintenance, and the educa-
" tion of your children? How many ſervants
" would you keep? How much would you re-
" ſerve for ſickneſs and unforeſeen expences ?
" How much would you conſecrate to the relief
" of the unfortunate and the public good ?—If
" your income depended either entirely or in part
" upon a tranſient advantage or a place which was
" not *aſſured* to you, how much would you expend
" annually? What ſum would you reſerve for form-
" ing a capital?" &c. &c. Prizes publicly given to
the beſt anſwers to queſtions of this kind would
conſtitute, in my opinion, an exerciſe equally engaging and more uſeful than the little comedies
and novels with which young perſons in the higher ſtations are generally entertained.

The honours conferred upon great men have
always appeared to me the moſt effectual means of
producing great men. I appoint, therefore, a
thouſand millions towards ſtriking medals, and
placing in the halls of all towns, or in any other
convenient places, ſtatues and buſts in honour of
ſuch great men as ſhall hereafter riſe up. I
deſire further that theſe honours be not paid them
till ten years after their deceaſe ; and that they be
decreed and proportioned by a tribunal compoſed
of ſuch upright, enlightened, and worthy citizens, as ſhall be moſt likely not to be dazzled by
falſe virtues.—It has been once reckoned, that
founding hoſpitals for the ſick is one of the beſt
public ſervices. For ſome years a conviction has
been

been gaining ground, that breathing the peſti-
lential air of hoſpitals doubles the danger of di-
ſeaſes; and that on this and other accounts they
probably *deſtroy* more lives than they *ſave*. I deſire, therefore, that 10,000 millions be employed
in eſtabliſhing in each pariſh of the kingdom
houſes of health, in which ſhall be maintained a
phyſician, a ſurgeon, and a convenient number
of ſiſters of charity and nurſes. Theſe houſes
ſhall ſupply the ſick *gratis* in their own houſes
with every aſſiſtance in food and medicine, and
none ſhall be taken to the houſe of health excepting thoſe whom it ſhall be impoſſible to aſſiſt at
home.

I have hitherto only directed the employment
of about two hundred thouſand millions. There
remain ſtill near *four millions of millions*, the appro-
priation of which I leave to the diſcretion of my
executors. I wiſh them to purchaſe and pull
down all ſuch houſes as incommode the public
way in all towns; to multiply ſquares, quays,
fountains, gardens, &c. in order to give ſalubrity
to the air of towns; to empty ponds; to clear
heaths; to deepen the beds of rivers ſo as to render
them navigable, and to unite them by means of
canals;—in a word, I wiſh them to co-operate in
every poſſible method with nature, which ſeems
to have deſigned *France* * to be the moſt delightful
country under heaven.

U 2

I hope

---

* FRANCE, undoubtedly, poſſeſſes ſome of the beſt *natural* advantages, and is a great kingdom. But it wants
the firſt of all advantages. It wants a free conſtitution of
government. It wants civil and religious liberty. BRITAIN
enjoys theſe bleſſings; and this, though leſs than a *fourth*
of FRANCE in extent and population, gives it a vaſt pre-
eminence. May theſe bleſſings be ſoon recovered by one of
theſe countries, and never loſt by the other.—*Tranſlator's
note.*

I hope that all good citizens will affift my executors in the choice of fuch ufeful eftablifhments
as fhall yet remain to be formed. I call upon
them to publifh the ideas with which patriotic
zeal may infpire them, fince now they are encouraged by the confoling certainty that funds
for executing them cannot be wanting.

I name for executors my deareft and beft friends
M. M. - - - - - - - - - - - [Here the teftator
names fix executors, who do not think proper at
prefent to reveal themfelves, and then goes on as
follows].

I beg of them to meet as often as the affairs of
my executorfhip fhall require. In cafe of an equal
divifion of opinions, the oldeft fhall have the caft-
ing vote. When one of them dies, I defire the
furvivors to fill the vacancy, as foon as may be,
with the moft honeft, zealous, and difinterefted
citizen of their acquaintance, and to proceed in
this manner for ever. I hope that during the firft
years of their executorfhip, when the operations
of the fund will be eafy, they will tranfact in this
bufinefs out of regard to me and to the public. I
forefee that, in procefs of time, the fums to be laid
out will become fo immenfely great, as to render
neceffary voyages and other confiderable expences,
which will be productive of no profit. For this
reafon I have left 125,000 livres of the fecond
fum unappropriated; of the third 711,000; and
of the fourth thirty-two millions. Thefe fums I
requeft them to accept as a compenfation for
their expences and trouble. I charge them always, as far as they can, without hazarding the
fecurity of the fund, to prefer thofe ways of laying out the accumulating fums which fhall be
moft ferviceable to individuals and the public.

If a reduction in the rate of intereft, or any un-
forefeen loffes, fhould injure the fund, fo as to re-

tard its increafe, the execution of my defires need
only be poftponed in proportion to the interrup-
tion that fhall happen.

May the fuccefs of thefe eftablifhments caufe
one day a few tears to be fhed on my grave. But
above all, may the example of an obfcure ihdivi-
dual * kindle the emulation of patriots, princes,
and public bodies; and engage them to give attention to this new but powerful and infallible
means of ferving pofterity, and contributing to
the future improvement and happinefs of the
world.

---

* During the printing of this Will, the *Gazette de France*
announced a legacy of the fame kind, which will prove to
our readers that thofe ideas may fometimes be realized.
" We read in fome of our papers a very fingular fact. Judge
" Normand, of Norwich, who died 1724, made a will, in
" which he bequeathed 4000l. fterling towards building in 60
" years, from that time, a charity fchool, to the founding
" of which the principal, and its accumulating intereft,
" during this period, fhould be appropriated.   His further
" difpofitions fix the number of fcholars to 120, regulates
" their meals for every day in the week, each to have for
" dinner on Sunday a pound of roaft beef, and in the even-
" ing ten ounces of plum-pudding.   He invefts the ma-
" nagement of this fchool in the Bifhop, the Chancellor,
" the Dean, the four members for the city and county, and
" eight clergymen.   The period determined upon for the
" execution of this Will expired in the month of May, and
" the accumulated fum amounts to 74,000l. fterling."
    Gazette de France, Friday, Aug. 13, 1784. No. 65.

TABLES.

T A B L E S.

No. I. *

TABLE *of the Produce of a Sum of* 100 *Livres,
with its accumulating Interest, during* 100 *Years,
at* 5 per Cent.

Years.	£.	s.	d.		Years.	£.	s.	d.
	100	—	—			115	15	3
	Int. 5	—	—			Int. 5	15	9
1	105	—	—		4	121	11	—
	5	5	0			6	1	6
2	110	5	—		5	127	12	6
	5	10	3			6	7	6
3	115	15	3		6	134	—	—

---

* RULE *for an easy Conversion of Livres into Pounds
Sterling.*

Strike off from the number of livres the two figures on
the right hand, and multiply by 4 the remaining figures.
The product increased by a *tenth* of itself will give nearly
the number of pounds answering to the number of livres.

Thus. 100,000 livres are equal nearly to 4000 multiplied
by 4, and the product (4000) increased by 400. That is,
they are equal to 4400 *l.*

In like manner, 1,725,768 livres are equal to 17,257
multiplied by 4, and the product (69,028) increased by
6902. That is, they are equal to 75,930 *l.*—*Translater.*
note.

Years.	£.	s.	d.		Years.	£.	s.	d.
	134	—	—			1145	14	—
Int.	6	14	—		Int.	57	5	6
7	140	14	—		51	1202	19	6
	7	—	6		&c.			
8	147	14	6		60	1866	3	—
	7	7	6			93	6	—
9	155	2	—		61	1959	9	—
	7	15	—		&c.			
10	162	17	—		70	3039	13	9
&c.						151	19	6
20	265	4	—		71	3191	13	3
	13	5	—		&c.			
21	278	9	—		80	4951	4	6
&c.						247	11	—
30	431	18	—		81	5198	15	6
	21	11	9		&c.			
31	453	9	9		90	8064	18	9
&c.						403	4	9
40	703	8	3		91	8468	3	6
	35	3	3		&c.			
41	738	11	6		99	12511	5	9
&c.						625	11	3
50	1145	14	—		100	13,136	17	—

OBSERVATIONS.

We found among the papers of the late *M.
Ricard* a great number of very curious tables, but
they

they have not been inserted here becaufe they had no direct relation to the object of his Will. He had computed the produce of a fum of 100 livres, with the accumulated intereft of 100 years, according to the different rates of intereft; and the refults varied much more than could be believed from the proportion of thofe different rates.

Intereft at 4 *per cent.* gives   50⎫
    at 5 *per cent.* —   131⎪ times the ori-
    at 6 *per cent.* —   339⎬ ginal fum.
    at 10 *per cent.* — 13,780⎭

From hence it follows, that if the operations are well managed, and the money laid out to advantage, even by finking the principal, (as is done in the fund for the 30 girls of Geneva) and converting afterwards the annual produce into capitals, the executors might confiderably accelerate the accomplifhment of the benevolent difpofitions of the teftator.

By laying out the money every three months, as is the cuftom in fome commercial places, the operations might alfo be accelerated, although but in a fmall degree.

REMARK, *by the* TRANSLATOR.

Thefe obfervations fhew that *M. Ricard* was himfelf poffeffed in a high degree of that knowledge of arithmetic which he has required in the comptrollers general (p. 139) as a condition of the redemption of the debts of *France*. In the laft paragraph, however, there is an incorrectnefs which fhews that he had not attended fufficiently to *one* circumftance in the improvement of money by compound intereft. This will appear from the following calculations.

One

One hundred livres will amount, if improved at 5 *per cent.* intereſt,

	Paid yearly. Livres.	Half-yearly. Livres.
In 100 years to	131,501	139,560
In 500 years to	3″,932,400 ,000,000—	5″,296,100′,000,000

Paid quarterly.

In 100 years to	143,890 livres.
In 500 years to	6″,166,000′000,000 livres.

By directing, therefore, that the laſt hundred livres ſhould be improved at 5 *per cent. quarterly* intereſt, M. *Ricard* might have gained an additional ſum equal to 2″,234,000 ,000,000 livres; that is, nearly equal to *a hundred thouſand millions* ſterling, which is a ſum more than ſufficient to encompaſs the earth with a belt of guineas all cloſe and five feet broad.

No. II.

TABLE *of the Produce of each Sum of* 100 *Livres, bequeathed by the Teſtator, from* one *hundred to* five *hundred Years.*

It has been proved by the preceding table, that a ſum of 100 livres, with the intereſt accumulating at 5 *per cent.* for 100 years, will produce 13,136 *liv.* 17 *ſous.* By multiplying this ſum by itſelf four times ſucceſſively, it will appear that the following ſums are the produce of each 100 livres at the end of each century.

	Liv.	ſous	den.
1ᵐᵒ. Produce of 100 livres, with the accumulated intereſt during 100 years -	13,136	17	—
2°. Produce of 100 livres, with the intereſt, during 200 years,	1,725,768	5	6
3°. Produce of 100 livres in 300 years - -	226,711,589	12	6
4°. Produce of 100 livres in 400 years - -	29,782,761,461	13	—
5°. Produce of 100 livres in 500 years - -	3,912,516,739,074	15	3

X   No. III.

No. III.

TABLE *of the Difpofition of the firft Sum, amounting to* 13,136 *livres* 17 *fous.*

	Livres	fous	den.
A prize of - - -	4,000	—	—
Three others of 600 livres each - -	1,800	—	—
An edition of the Prize Difcourfe, extracts from the three others, with 50,000 copies	7,336	17	—
Total	13,136	17	—

No. IV.

TABLE *of the Difpofition of the fecond Sum, a-
mounting to* 1,725,768 *livres* 5 *fous* 6 *den.*

	Livres	fous	den.
A fund for 80 prizes of 100 livres each,	1,600,000	—	—
Referved towards defraying the expences of the executors, - -	125,768	5	6
Total	1,725,768	5	6

No. V.

TABLE *of the Difpofition of the third Sum, amounting to* 226,711,589 *liv.* 12 *fous* 6 *den.*

	Livres	fous	den.
Five hundred patriotic banks for lend-ing money without intereft -	196,000,000	—	—
Building 12 mufeums at 500,000 liv. each - 6,000,000			
Fund for an annual income of 100,000 livres for each mufe-um - - 24,000,000	30,000,000	—	—
Referved towards defraying the expences of the executors - -	711,589	12	6
Total	226,711,589	12	6

During the three years employed in building
the mufeums, the income of 100,000 livres is to be
laid by, towards purchafing the library, the cabinets,

binets, the carriages, the horfes, and all the furni-
ture of the mufeum. Afterwards it is to be employed as follows.

	Livres.
Table-expences for the 40 members of the mufe-um, the fix fecretaries, the defigner, the en-graver, and all the domeftics, coachmen, cooks, gardeners, &c.	50,000
Salaries of the fecretaries, defigner, engraver, and wages of the domeftics,	12,000
Expences of the ftable and carriages,	10,000
The library and cabinets,	10,000
Repairs of the building and furniture,	8,000
Printing and unforefeen expences,	10,000

Total 100,000

No. VI.

TABLE *of the Difpofition of the 4th Sum, amounting
to* 29,782,761,461 *liv.* 13 *fous.*

Towards building 100 towns, containing each of
them 150,000 fouls.

In order that thefe towns may be wholefome and convenient,
it will be proper to confecrate to each of them a very large
circular piece of ground, containing 6000 acres ; which being eftimated at the higheft, may be valued at 1000 livres
each acre. By judging from the towns which now exift,
there will not be required more than from 4 to 5000 houfes
for 150,000 inhabitants ; but it is not conducive to the
health of mankind, to be fo crowded together. I fuppofe
then that each of thefe towns may contain 7500 houfes *,
which, one with the other, will coft 35000 livres in building. Each town will coft

	Livres.	fous.
Six thoufand acres of ground at 1000 livres per acre	6,000,000	—
7,500 houfes, at 35,000 livres each houfe	262,500,000	—
Public buildings, town houfes, bridges, churches, &c.	29,000,000	—
Total	297,500,000	—

* It would have been much better if *M. Ricard* had allowed a houfe for every family, which would have made the
number of houfes about 30000.

The

	Livres.	fous.

The preceding fum multiplied into 100,
gives   -   -   -   29,750,000,000 —
Referved towards defraying the ex-
pences of the executors,   -   32,761,461 13

Total, 29,782,761,461 13

No. VII.

TABLE *of the Difpofition of the 5th Sum, amounting
to* 3,912,516,739,074 *liv.* 15 *fous* 3 *den.*

The national debt of France,   - 6 thoufand millions.
————————— of England, 12
A fund towards dividing annually
15 hundred thoufand livres a-
mong the pacific powers of Europe,   -   -   30
A fimilar diftribution among all
the powers of the world,   - 100
Abolition of lotteries,   -   1
Extinction of ufelefs offices,   -   1
Suppreffion of venality in offices of
of importance,   -   1
A domaine to be offered to his Ma-
jefty,   -   -   -   1
A fund to be employed in annui-
ties and penfions,   -   2
An addition to the fettled ftipends
of the clergy,   -   1
Allowance to children under three
years of age,   -   -   -   2
A foundation for 500,000 fmall *free-
holds* with commodious cottages, 4
Enfranchifement of vaffals,   -   2
Foundations for houfes of educati-
on for the people,   -   6
Houfes of induftry,   -   20
Afylums for penitent young women, 1
Hofpitals of Angels,   -   2
Statues, bufts, and public honours, 1
Houfes of health,   -   10

Total of appropriated fums, 203
Remain unappropriated,   3,709,516,739,074 15 3

Total, 3,912,516,739,074 15 3

F I N I S.

www.ingramcontent.com/pod-product-compliance
Ingram Content Group UK Ltd.
Pitfield, Milton Keynes, MK11 3LW, UK
UKHW042152280225
455719UK00001B/296

9 781108 060172